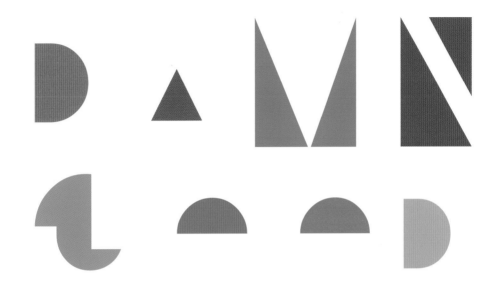

For more excellent books and resources for designers, visit www.howdesign.com.

15 14 13 12 11   5 4 3 2 1

ISBN-13: 978-1-4403-1548-0

Distributed in Canada by Fraser Direct
100 Armstrong Avenue
Georgetown, Ontario, Canada L7G 5S4
Tel: (905) 877-4411

Distributed in the U.K. and Europe by F&W Media International, LTD
Brunel House, Forde Close, Newton Abbot, TQ12 4PU, UK
Tel: (+44) 1626 323200, Fax: (+44) 1626 323319
Email: enquiries@fwmedia.com

Distributed in Australia by Capricorn Link
P.O. Box 704, Windsor, NSW 2756 Australia
Tel: (02) 4577-3555

Damn Good is set in P22 Bifur and Aller.

Bifur was originally designed by Adolphe Mouron Cassandre in 1929 and adapted into its current form, P22 Bifur, by Richard Keglar in 2004.

Aller was designed in 2008 by Henrik Birkvig, Dalton Maag, Bruno Maag, Marc Weyman, and Ron Carpenter, originally for the Danish School of Media and Journalism.

Designed by Hexanine (www.Hexanine.com)
Author photographs by Brendan Shanley (www. LostInPrint.com)
Production coordinated by Crescent Hill Books (www.CrescentHillBooks.com)

DAMN GOOD

TOP DESIGNERS DISCUSS THEIR ALL-TIME FAVORITE PROJECTS

TIM LAPETINO + JASON ADAM

HEXANINE

HOW
BOOKS

Cincinnati, Ohio
www.howdesign.com

CONTENTS

THANKS

No one creates in isolation, and we could not have authored this book alone.
We are indebted to a host of people, and though that list is undoubtedly longer
than the one below, we wholeheartedly give thanks, props, and shouts for all the love,
support, and encouragement that came our way during the course of creating this book.

In no particular order...

To Nancy Heinonen, our awesome producer.

To Megan Lane Patrick and the rest of the team at HOW Books,
for letting us be ourselves, and embracing us thusly.

To Emily Lapetino, the best wife ever, and one of the
greatest cheerleaders for Hexanine from the opening bell on.

To Brendan Shanley, for deeply improving on reality.

To Love Ablan, for your friendship, keen eye, and charming wit.

To all of the generous designers who submitted their work.
Your stories and creativity fueled this book.

To all of our great clients at Hexanine who have challenged,
partnered with, and worked alongside us through the years.
This book is rooted in our collaborations with you, both past and future.

And to Janet, Bob, Frank, and Jackie—you know what you did.

INTRO
DUCTION

Everyone has their favorites.

Favorite TV shows, favorite colors, favorite sweatpants. But for designers of all stripes, the term *favorite* can also bleed into our projects. Even though we're often working alongside (and at the behest of) others, this craft ends up tugging at our emotions. The work we do sometimes takes on special meaning, and over the course of a career, any designer worth her salt can easily rattle off her all-time favorite projects.

That's what this book is all about. Not *just* the best looking, highest profile, or smartest work strategically—but a combination of all those factors coalescing into the nebulous designation of *favorite*. That hard-to-measure factor is the foundation of the book you're holding in your hands.

Of course, there still might be a question lingering in the frontal lobe of your cerebrum: What makes a piece of design "damn good?"

Our attempt to answer that question is at the heart of this book. In selecting work for inclusion in *Damn Good*, we focused on a couple of specific ingredients that breed favorite work—passion and inspiration.

Passion is the critical need to put the best possible work out there, loudly and proudly. Not just a whisper, but a battle cry of designers investing thought, strategy, emotion, and heart into the work they do. It's being able to say, "DAMN, I'm proud of what I've done"—and wanting the world to see it.

As far as inspiration, our rule of thumb in designing and curating this book was this: if it moved us, got us grooving, or challenged our perceptions, we wanted to include it—because it inspired us. We tried our *damnedest* to push the boundaries of the typical, to capture work in a variety of design disciplines, finally gathering a collection that stands apart.

We really wanted to provide a wide view of the fantastic design that's happening all over the world. The work between these covers spans 35 countries, and we dug deep to find not only great projects by well-known, successful firms—but also to ferret out the creative juices flowing in undiscovered corners, away from the spotlight.

This is a book of work that turns us on. And these stimuli have their origins all over the globe, from China, to Croatia, Mexico, New Zealand, the UK, the States, and many other points on the map. Designers and creatives from all of these places submitted their best, most favorite work and talked about it. ▶

The work between these covers spans 35 countries, and we dug deep to find not only great projects by well-known, successful firms—but also to ferret out the creative juices flowing in undiscovered corners, away from the spotlight.

THE CUTTING ROOM FLOOR

Some work never sees the light of day. Whether it's because of company politics, changes in management, or plain, old client dislike, great concepts are often buried. But we believe that axed work is often instructive and inspirational, and worth another look. The icon above appears periodically throughout this book, denoting work that we've rescued from the cutting room floor.

In the pages that follow, these creators opened up about process, creativity, design goals, and even projects that ended up on the cutting room floor—all in their own words. We believe this tangible, human perspective on the creative journey is what makes damn good work Damn Good.

Since this book is rooted in the work that moves us—we'd be silly not to mention some of the work of others that has grabbed us over the years, with its stunning combo of passion and inspiration.

1 *Bat Manga*, book designer Chip Kidd's bizarre and amazing jaunt into Japanese interpretation of the 1960s era Batman. The concept is outlandish, the layouts are powerfully wacked, and the whole package is executed with a manic pop energy and panache that we can't help but love.

2 The late George Oppenheimer designed this logo for the video game company, Atari. Both timeless and unmistakably 1980s, this logo conjures up childhood memories of Chuck E. Cheese's pizza, and laying on the basement floor, playing Missile Command on our Atari 2600s.

3 It's easy to dismiss the H&R Block identity as a simple green block. And it *is* just a green block—but therein lies the genius of it (not to mention Landor's rockstar work in selling the concept to their client). It's appropriate,

memorable, and its true excellence shines in the amazing applications, where it gains true life and personality.

4 Long-time Beatles pal Klaus Voorman created this proto-psychedelic hand-drawn cover for the group's 1966 album *Revolver*. Unapologetically stark and surreal, this collage/illustration was the perfect avant-garde introduction to the eclectic and changing Beatles sounds within.

5 It might seem simple now, but Polaroid's rainbow colored packaging was an epiphany and a major differentiator versus the stalwart Kodak Company when Paul Giambarba designed it in 1958. Bold, simple, elegant, modern, and approachable.

6 The Sprint logo might be the perfect synergy of disparate brand elements. This identity redesign came in the wake of Sprint's merger with Nextel. The designers managed to meld the great, historical "pin drop" symbol of Sprint, with the bold brand equity of Nextel's yellow. Simply great.

When it's all said and done, each of the pieces we've included in this book is a signpost on the way to the place where passion and inspiration drive us all. Let's get there together. ■

Tim Lapetino & Jason Adam
Chicago, IL, October 2011

1

2

H&R BLOCK

3

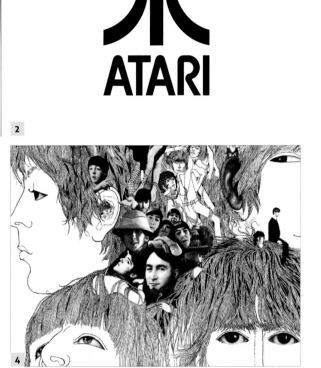

4

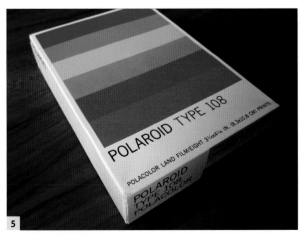

5

6

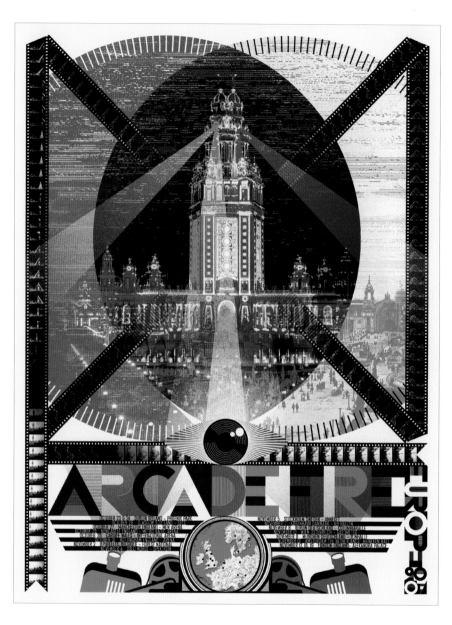

The eye, cameras, and spotlight imply always being watched and on camera in modern society.

Arcade Fire
Europe Tour Poster

"I've had a continuing relationship with Arcade Fire since 2004 as their primary poster designer. The posters are printed in-house at our own print shop then sent straight out to the locations on tour. This design was a favorite of mine, using imagery from the Pan-American Expo from 1901. I used screen captures of old film and placed them one by one to create the 'X' on this poster. The eye, cameras, and spotlight imply always being watched and on camera in modern society." —WW

■ FIRM **Burlesque of North America**, Minneapolis, MS, USA
■ CREATIVE TEAM **Wes Winship**
■ CLIENT **Arcade Fire**

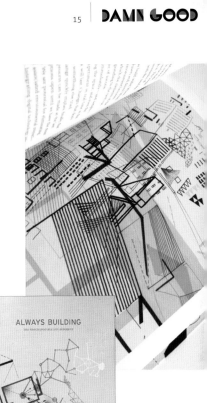

ACHIEVING THE PROMISE   83

■ ■ ■

Herman Miller: Always Building

"I was approached by People Design and was so excited to be given a brief to work with one of my favorite companies, Herman Miller. Charles and Ray Eames, who worked with Herman Miller to make their most iconic furniture creations, are some of my biggest design idols. To be indirectly connected to them through this project was a great honor. I love trying to communicate abstract thoughts and experiments such as this. It enables the creative process and allows me to explore all sorts of directions, pulling in all sorts of visual and mental references into the final piece." —*JGH*

■ FIRM **James Gulliver Hancock**, New York, NY, USA
■ CREATIVE TEAM **James Gulliver Hancock**, **Brian Hauch**
■ CLIENT **Herman Miller**

On D-Day it was very interesting to watch people handle the booklet.

Završnica, Booklet for Beckett's *Endgame*

"This booklet for Samuel Barclay Beckett's play, *Endgame*, was commissioned, designed, and printed in six days. I am very fond of this design, because it is proof that in most cases, the first idea is the best one. The design was done on my father's computer in his office. I had only the basic fonts, little from my archive, and no camera. So the design was the happy result of circumstances. The deadline was "yesterday," so I also worked on its printing and folding. It was folded manually, and even the printer's wife came to help us. The design follows the director's intention to connect three major occurrences in his interpretation of the play—the 20th anniversary of Beckett's death, the fall of the Berlin Wall, and the breakdown of Socialism in Eastern Europe." *—MJ*

■ FIRM **Marivo**, Osijek, Croatia
■ CREATIVE TEAM **Marko Jovanovac**
■ CLIENT **Osijek Summer of Culture**

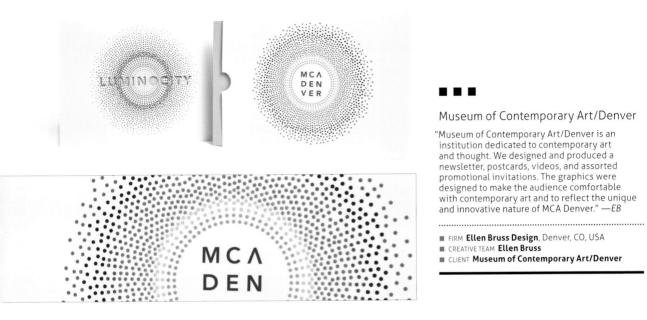

■ ■ ■

Museum of Contemporary Art/Denver

"Museum of Contemporary Art/Denver is an institution dedicated to contemporary art and thought. We designed and produced a newsletter, postcards, videos, and assorted promotional invitations. The graphics were designed to make the audience comfortable with contemporary art and to reflect the unique and innovative nature of MCA Denver." —EB

- FIRM **Ellen Bruss Design**, Denver, CO, USA
- CREATIVE TEAM **Ellen Bruss**
- CLIENT **Museum of Contemporary Art/Denver**

■ ■ ■

Walla Walla Chamber Music Festival Posters

"This project was for violinist/founder Timothy Christie. In 2009, I created the first poster, an illustration of Brahms, using stencil and sumi ink. After that, Tim decided to keep the project going, letting us know which classical composer the festival would highlight each year, and I ran wild with the themes. It's been fun to experiment with different media, too—along with sumi ink and stencil, I've used a handmade bamboo stick pen with Beethoven, crayons for Mozart, and for 2012, a collage of Schubert's face." —SO

- FIRM **Modern Dog Design Co.**, Seattle, WA, USA
- CREATIVE TEAM **Shogo Ota**
- CLIENT **Walla Walla Chamber Music Festival**

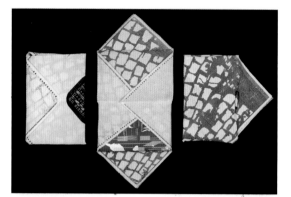

The 7th Macao Design Biennial Archive

"This is the 'catalog' of the 7th Macao Design Biennial, and while a catalog usually takes the form of a book, this design is composed of nine individual pieces which can be rearranged, forming a unique experience with each combination. The winning entries from different regions are displayed on a Portuguese-style pebbled plaza, under the bright sunlight. The giant 'Archive' is also made out of nine pieces of artwork." —KC

■ FIRM **Joaquim Cheong Design**, Macao S.A.R., Macao
■ CREATIVE TEAM **Kuokwai Cheong**, **Houiok Lai**
■ CLIENT **Macao Designers Association**

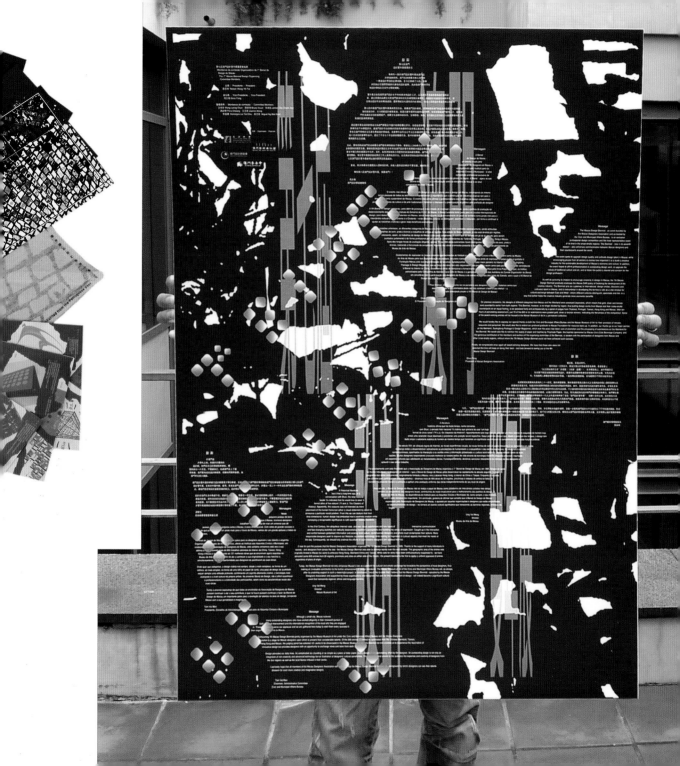

A History

LENNARD J. DAVIS

■ ■

My first attempts at
computer generated
obsessive lettering
were failures—the
repetition had to
be done by hand
to be truly obsessive.

■ ■

■ ■ ■

Obsession Book Cover

"This wide ranging history traces how
the concept of obsession has changed
over time, and how obsession has been
perceived in both positive (professional
dedication, romantic devotion) and
negative ways (OCD, nymphomania).
Rather than depict any one of these
myriad forms of obsession, I decided to
let the cover itself be a product of an
obsessive process. My first attempts at
computer generated obsessive lettering
were failures—the repetition had to
be done by hand to be truly obsessive.
Lauren Nassef (my wife, illustrator, and
frequent collaborator) suggested a pin
prick technique she had used years
ago. I prepared a type treatment which
Lauren then punched out of heavy
card with a pin, hole-by-hole." —*IT*

■ FIRM **The University of Chicago Press**, Chicago, IL, USA
■ CREATIVE TEAM **Isaac Tobin**, **Lauren Nassef**, **Jill Shimabukuro**
■ CLIENT **The University of Chicago Press**

■ All Access: The Making of Thirty
■ Extraordinary Graphic Designers

■ "This book serves as a 'Behind the Music' for
graphic design, telling the life stories of 30
amazing designers, and featuring samples of
work spanning their entire careers, not just
the glossy, successful stuff." —SGB

■ FIRM **344 Design, LLC**, Pasadena, CA, USA
■ CREATIVE TEAM **Stefan G. Bucher**
■ CLIENT **Rockport Books**

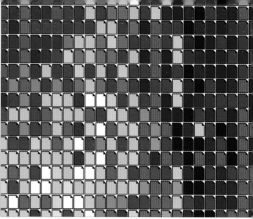

Unisource 20th Anniversary Poster

"To celebrate Unisource Chicago's 20th Paper Show, AIGA Chicago asked a number of designers to each create a poster. The theme 'twenty' was open to interpretation— 20 years, 20 paper shows, 20 anything. But twenty anything doesn't make a good poster. It needed a few constraints. So to 'twenty' we added 'paper.' The single biggest change in the design and paper industry in the last twenty years has been digital technology. The end of paper was often heard but never seen. No doubt things have changed but paper remains vital. So, what if we substituted the pixel with paper? 14,784 tinted paper icons later, we had our digital '20' made of 'paper.'" —*TB*

- FIRM **lowercase**, Chicago, IL, USA
- CREATIVE TEAM **Tim Bruce**
- CLIENT **AIGA Chicago and Unisource**

To 33.4% of the population in Karnataka, garbage is fashion. **Please donate your old clothes.** New Ark Mission of India. 98452 81915. www.newarkmission.org

■ ■ ■

Winter Collection Campaign

"The winter months are the ones that take the most violent toll on India's poor. After long hot summers, the poor are really not ready for the extreme cold that follows. For this project, we dressed street kids in their usual everyday clothes (made from discarded newspapers, sacking, cardboard) and photographed them walking the ramp. This juxtaposition of the usual in an unusual setting startled people and woke them up. The campaign was executed as a series of posters and standees in corporate offices and churches. The client was hoping for 3,500 donated sets of clothes. However, they were overwhelmed when they received over 6,000 sets of clothes." —*SR*

■ FIRM **Ogilvy**, Bangalore, Karnataka, India
■ CREATIVE TEAM **Siju RS**, **Senthil Kumar**, **Gautam Dev**, **Neel Roy**
■ CLIENT **New Ark Mission Of India**

■ ■ ■

Mohawk Solutions Promotion

"A paper promotion is one of those dream jobs many designers hope to do at some point in their career, even in these (supposed) waning days of print. What made the Solutions promotion both fun and challenging is that the creative brief was exactly that—brief. Mohawk asked us to create a teaching guide aimed at in-house design teams, corporate materials, and projects on a budget, but otherwise left the design and specific content entirely up to us. We randomly selected ten images and intuitively compiled them into a sequence that would repeat three times. Next, we gave the sequence to three writers who each wrote their own original narrative to accompany it. Finally, we designed to each written piece while still maintaining the same image layout throughout all three sequences. It's the 'Groundhog Day' paper promotion—it always starts in the same place, but the three 'solutions' are different." —*EH*

■ FIRM **Volume Inc.**, San Francisco, CA, USA
■ CREATIVE TEAM **Eric Heiman**, **Adam Brodsley**, **Talin Wadsworth**
■ CLIENT **Mohawk Fine Papers**

He gave me about
7,000 photos taken
on set, and I spent
the next few months
editing those down
to this large book.

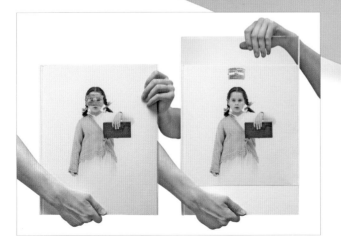

■ The Fall by Tarsem (Book)

"Tarsem asked me to create an object
he could use to present his movie,
The Fall, to potential distributors
without having to show them the
actual film, which he was still editing
at the time. He gave me about 7,000
photos taken on set, and I spent
the next few months editing those down
to this large book. In this movie the
little girl wears a paper mask every
time she enters her fantasy world.
At Tarsem's suggestion, we had that
mask silk-screened on a custom vinyl
sleeve, so you'd take it off her face
when you opened the book." —*SGB*

■ FIRM **344 Design, LLC**, Pasadena, CA, USA
■ CREATIVE TEAM **Stephen Berkman**, **Steven Colover**, **Tarsem**, **Stefan G. Bucher**
■ CLIENT **Googly Films**

We created a card that engages the recipient with a little interactivity and highlights the salon's services.

Impact Salon Business Cards

"The only input we received for this project was, 'Make it cool.' By creating a sleeve, we were able to tuck an appointment card inside, and had fun with the details, like making the map out of scissor shears. We created a card that engages the recipient with a little interactivity and highlights the salon's services. There are two separate cards, representing male and female clientele. As the appointment card is pulled out of the sleeve, the hair changes. The man gets a dye job and the woman gets highlights and curls. The cards are high-fashion yet functional and further the salon's mid-century brand." —RC

■ FIRM **Creative Suitcase**, Austin, TX, USA
■ CREATIVE TEAM **Rachel Clemens**, **Jennifer James Wright**
■ CLIENT **Impact Salon**

Lacoste Footwear Posters

"The posters we designed for Lacoste's line of footwear were used in retail locations to drive brand awareness and feature new products. The visual treatments draw inspiration from the design of the shoes and turn it up to eleven. This mixture of pop kitsch and modern layouts adds a feeling of playfulness that is a natural match for Lacoste's offerings." —*JBC*

- FIRM **The O Group**, New York, NY, USA
- CREATIVE TEAM **Jason B. Cohen**, **J. Kenneth Rothermich**, **Katie Mangano**
- CLIENT **Pentland**

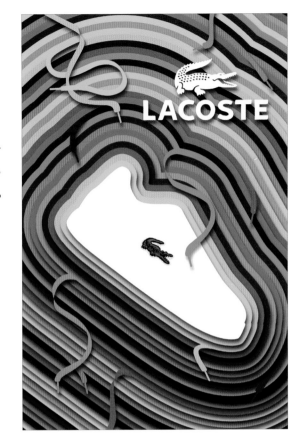

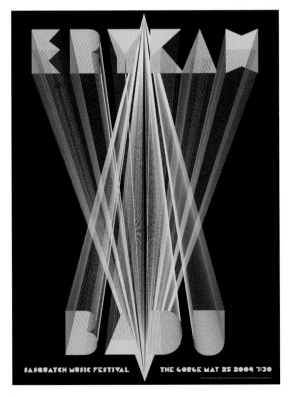

Erykah Badu

"Erykah Badu is a neo-soul singer who merges the funk of the 1970s and 1980s with a futuristic aesthetic. The majority of her posters, album covers, and other merchandise uses a similar aesthetic—swirly, hand-drawn lettering, reminiscent of the 1970s. For this poster for her performance at the Sasquatch Music Festival, the lettering emphasizes the synthesized futurism in her music, while still giving a nod to the playful funk and soul that holds it all together." —*JO*

- FIRM **Weather Control**, Seattle, WA, USA
- CREATIVE TEAM **Josh Oakley**
- CLIENT **Erykah Badu**

Design This Day: 8 Decades of Influential Design

■ FIRM **Turnstyle**, Seattle, WA, USA
■ CREATIVE TEAM **Ben Graham**, **Steven Watson**, **Jason Gómez**, **Bryan Mamaril**
■ CLIENT **Teague**

■ ■

The subject matter
was fantastic.
It was a treat to be
able to design for,
and about, design.

■ ■

Steve Watson,
*Principal/Creative Director,
Turnstyle*

■
■ **Why does this project exist?**
■ *Steve Watson: Design This Day: 8 Decades of Influential Design* is a limited edition book created to commemorate the 80th anniversary of Seattle product design firm Teague. The book is a compilation of Teague's own work as well as their perspective on the industry's most inspired, thoughtful, striking, and even amusing designs.

Teague wanted to create a book as both a historical retrospective celebrating eight decades of design and as a forward-looking thought piece about where the industry is going. A key objective was to help re-establish Teague's reputation as a major player and innovator in the industrial design industry. The book was to be a gift for attendees of their 80th anniversary party as well as for new and potential clients as a business development tool.

The book's pages showcase Teague's industrial design projects in photos, thumbnail sketches, and original illustrations. It even contains a section of embarrassing projects Teague worked on over the past eighty years, including concepts for an invisible dress and a hair-growing machine.

Let us in on the story of your client, Teague.
SW: Raymond Loewy, Henry Dreyfuss, and Walter Dorwin Teague wrote the book on 20th century industrial design—literally. (In fact, Teague authored an extensive treatise on the state of design in the late 1930s entitled *Design This Day*, which we referenced in the title for the current edition.) Teague and his contemporaries were out there building the discipline—experimenting with design to support new needs and the growing sophistication of consumers. Times changed, but it turns out that Wally's ideals were not too far off base. The principles on which he built his firm are as relevant today as ever, as the world is embracing the full power of design to help solve societal and commercial challenges, and to drive positive change.

What was your favorite part of this project?
SW: This was a dream project for us for several reasons. First, because of the collaborative nature of the project. The entire organization, content, and form of the book was the result of collaboration among Turnstyle, Teague, and the writers. This early participation in the concept development helped not only inform the graphic design, but also allowed us substantial leeway in ▶

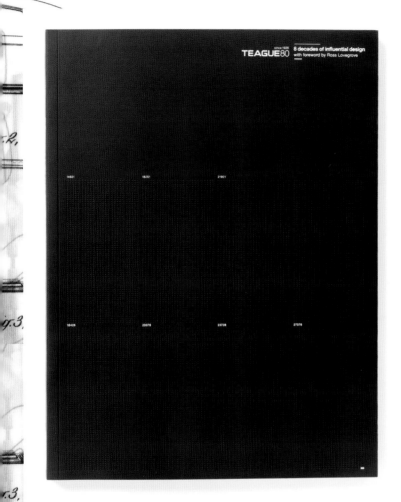

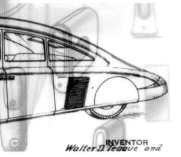

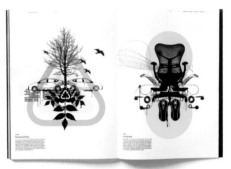

The Turnstyle team had the luxury of working with an archivist to select material from among Teague's rich design archives for the book.

The more a client allows us to inject our art direction, voice, and authorship into a piece, the more rewarding it is for us, and the more it tends to stand out.

This was a dream project for us because of the collaborative nature of the project. The entire organization, content, and form of the book was the result of collaboration among Turnstyle, Teague, and the writers.

developing the structure of the book. The collaborative process included working with an archivist, and pouring through treasure troves of design imagery. Furthermore, the project was large enough in scope that it allowed (even necessitated) all the designers in our office to collaborate together on the design. We all generated multiple layouts and ideas for the feel of the book.

Secondly, the CEO of Teague is an ideal client—someone who is truly passionate about what he does and has a compelling story to tell. He was looking to stretch aesthetically and conceptually in order to communicate that Teague was reemerging as a major player. It was incredibly satisfying and empowering working with a client/decision-maker who understands and appreciates design's role in elevating communications.

Finally, the subject matter was fantastic. It was a treat to be able to design for, and about, design. Who wouldn't want to have some of the most iconic industrial design examples of the past century as the tent stakes for the content of their book?

Why does this entry stand out from other work you've done?
SW: Probably because of its very nature as a design-driven book about design. Its ridiculously high production value—

including varied use of paper stocks and printing techniques—sets it apart. And the fact that we not only designed the book, but helped conceptualize, curate, and write so much of the content sets it apart.

The more a client allows us to inject our art direction, voice, and authorship into a piece, the more rewarding it is for us, and the more it tends to stand out.

Were there any difficulties along the way?
SW: Curating and organizing all the varied content were both the most challenging aspects and the aspects that drove what is unique about the project. Digging through old photo albums and countless boxes of glass slides for that one nugget of content was tedious at times, but also had an aspect of anthropology/archaeology that was exciting and rewarding.

Tell us about the production of the book.
SW: We used a variety of production techniques in different sections of the book—including the finicky blind debossed, dual-foil stamped, gate-folded, soft-touch cover. Also, there are exactly 29,200 blind-embossed dots on the cover of the book, one for each day Teague had been in business as it commemorated its 80th anniversary. The tactile effect on the Fibermark Touché paper (which on its own feels something like neoprene rubber) is incredibly satisfying.

Our first loves are print and packaging. There's something about the tactile qualities of paper and ink and material that connects with us. Interestingly, we feel like print is diminishing, but becoming more valuable at the same time. ■

Iron Man Covers

"To illustrate writer Matt Fraction's story arc in which Tony Stark (Iron Man) wipes his mind in order to prevent information falling into the wrong hands, a stripped-down aesthetic was employed. Inset illustrations describe the turmoil inside Tony's head. I mocked up the first two using elements from Salvador's previous work on the title to illustrate what I was after, and then he ran with the concept and gave me exactly what I was hoping for. These covers came in second in the Best Covers of 2010 by MTV, and they stood out strongly against the busy and brash covers of the average superhero books on the racks." —RH

■ FIRM **Device, Inc.**, London, UK
■ CREATIVE TEAM **Rian Hughes**, **Salvador Larocca**
■ CLIENT **Marvel Comics**

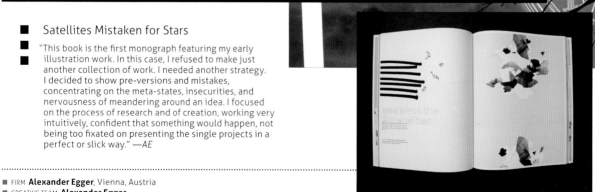

- Satellites Mistaken for Stars

"This book is the first monograph featuring my early illustration work. In this case, I refused to make just another collection of work. I needed another strategy. I decided to show pre-versions and mistakes, concentrating on the meta-states, insecurities, and nervousness of meandering around an idea. I focused on the process of research and of creation, working very intuitively, confident that something would happen, not being too fixated on presenting the single projects in a perfect or slick way." —AE

- FIRM **Alexander Egger**, Vienna, Austria
- CREATIVE TEAM **Alexander Egger**
- CLIENT **Rupa Publishing**

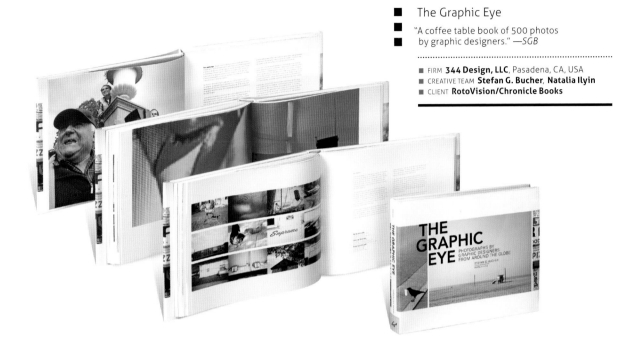

■ **The Graphic Eye**
■
■ "A coffee table book of 500 photos
by graphic designers." —*SGB*

....

■ FIRM **344 Design, LLC**, Pasadena, CA, USA
■ CREATIVE TEAM **Stefan G. Bucher**, **Natalia Ilyin**
■ CLIENT **RotoVision/Chronicle Books**

■ ■ ■

AIGA Holiday Mailer

"To promote AIGA DC/Timsco Screensprinting's workshop, we satirized DC's unique political climate by creating a silkscreen design that was a spoof on political leanings. ('Left' was on the right, and 'right' was on the left.) We also showcased the printer's ability to print on unique surfaces by choosing printed newspapers (each was different) as the paper stock. And finally, we folded the paper, added a printed post-it note, to kid about the practice of sending colleagues articles of interest from the newspaper." —*BS*

....

■ FIRM **Beth Singer Design**, Arlington, VA, USA
■ CREATIVE TEAM **Howard Smith**, **Beth Singer**,
Sucha Snidvongs, **Peter Schwartz**
■ CLIENT **AIGA DC**

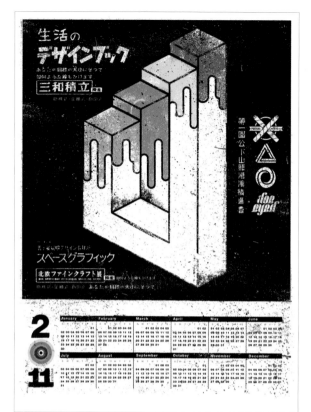

Doe Eyed Calendar

"At the end of 2010, we were obsessed with Japanese modern design. We salivated over every Japanese poster or book that came out of the 1960s and 1970s. When it came time to create our self-promo materials for the year, it was only natural to combine Japanese modernism with our love of optical illusions. Most of the Japanese writing is nonsense stolen from old horror/slasher films, so modern + eye tricks + horror = a perfect summation of the Doe Eyed experience." —EN

■ FIRM **Doe Eyed**, Lincoln, NE, USA
■ CREATIVE TEAM **Eric Nyffeler**, **Michael Nielsen**
■ CLIENT **Self-Promotion**

Bitef Theater Festival Visual Pitch

"For this Bitef creative pitch, the theme of the year was 'in search of identity' and the two projects I created represent my view on the theme. This first one is about a search of identity in ourselves, starting with our own identities, and the second one takes a deconstructive approach of searching inside Bitef." —VS

■ FIRM **Vjeko Sumic Design**, Belgrade, Serbia
■ CREATIVE TEAM **Vjeko Sumic**
■ CLIENT **44. BITEF FESTIVAL**

CUTTING
ROOM
FLOOR

Neenah Paper 1/2 The Job

"*1/2 the Job* reintroduces Neenah Paper's Classic grades in a new and modern way, by demonstrating how fine paper can dramatically change the look and feel of a business identity. Any design and the material it's printed on should work together, and *1/2 the Job* showcases just that idea. A great design on the computer screen is only 1/2 the job. For creativity to really communicate, you've got to touch it. Feel it. " —DS

- FIRM **And Partners**, New York, NY, USA
- CREATIVE TEAM **David Schimmel**, **Albert Ignacio**, **Joseph Cohen**
- CLIENT **Neenah Paper**

House of the Golden Fleece Book

"*Since 1904: House of the Golden Fleece* is a beautifully printed book archiving the history of the I. Spiewak & Sons, Inc. fashion brand. The goal was to convey a metaphorical theme of building and the literal term *fashion house*. To illustrate this concept, an architectural theme was used throughout the publication, with original mid-century factory blueprints adorning the front and back covers. These images are accented by House Industries' Neutra Dispay Drafting typeface. The interior content was hand picked from century-old archives stored in Spiewak's Mississippi Factory, which is still in operation today. It's a fascinating look at the growth of one of America's oldest family-operated companies." —ML

- FIRM **Michelle LeClerc Design**, Los Angeles, CA, USA
- CREATIVE TEAM **Michelle LeClerc**, **Josh Chapman**
- CLIENT **I. Spiewak & Sons**

LOVE HELSINKI Coaster Collection

"*LOVE HELSINKI* is a collection of twelve different coasters illustrating various aspects of our home town—things and places that we feel make it Helsinki. I love how the set functions like a small art exhibition. It's also a great game to play while having friends over, trying to guess which place or thing each of the coasters represents!" —*LS*

FIRM **Laura Suuronen**, Helsinki, Finland
CREATIVE TEAM **Laura Suuronen**, **Vesa Ahtiainen**, **Anssi Räisänen**
CLIENT **LOVE HELSINKI**

From the beginning, I had a picture in my mind: the final book as a big batch of paper between two rough, cardboard covers—a working tool rather than a coffee table book.

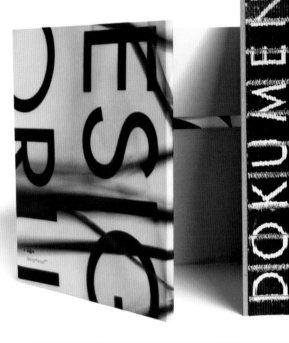

Dokument: Designforum Vienna 2006–2010

"This project was very challenging and complicated because of the tight schedule and the variety of materials from many different sources. From the beginning, I had a picture in my mind: the final book as a big batch of paper between two rough, cardboard covers—a working tool rather than a coffee table book. We played with the medium of paper, creating abstract paper constructions for the chapter pages that added a playful aspect to the analytic and scientific content. It also seemed to work well for the audience: We won design awards and got a lot of recognition for this project." —AE

■ FIRM **Alexander Egger**, Vienna, Austria
■ CREATIVE TEAM **Alexander Egger**, **Isolde Fitzel**
■ CLIENT **Designforum Vienna**

■ Don't Let Haiti Get Lost in the Cracks Posters

■
■ "As the shock and devastation of Haiti's plight fades from
■ the headlines, its vibrant people and culture are still in ruin.
'Don't Let Haiti Get Lost in the Cracks' is part of a nationwide
poster campaign to support the relief effort and remind us that
the people of Haiti still need our help. These posters focus on
the spirit and humanity of what happier times for the country
held in the past—and are still to come." —JR

■ FIRM **Brunet-García Advertising & PR**, Jacksonville, FL, USA
■ CREATIVE TEAM **Jefferson Rall**
■ CLIENT **Haiti Poster Project**

AIGA LA
Speakeasy

Honoring AIGA LA 2010 Fellows
and Celebrating all AIGA LA
Fellows and Medalists
past and present

JOHN COY ⋆ JERI HEIDEN

*Enjoy an unprecedented evening of unique conversations and merriment
at the AIGA's modern-day speakeasy event at the Palihouse West Hollywood.
January 20, 6:30-9:30pm · tickets & details: aigalosangeles.org/events*

■ ■

I think it's really cool
when visual work has so
much motion to it that it
practically tells you how
it will come to life.

■ ■

■ ■ ■

AIGA LA: Speakeasy Poster

"For AIGA LA's annual Fellows
celebration, I teamed up with Jared
Purrington, who illustrated this
lovely mandala of Los Angeles
landmarks. Using this concept, we
created a poster that would serve
as key art for the event. Since the
fellows honored at the event were
largely print designers, the ink is
a nod to printing ink. The art is so
versatile that another designer was
able to animate it spinning, and
building itself outward, splattered
with ink and dripping down to form
the names of the honorees." —HP

■ FIRM **Parlato Design Studio**, Los Angeles, CA, USA
■ CREATIVE TEAM **Heather Parlato, Melanie Paykos, Jared Purrington**
■ CLIENT **AIGA Los Angeles**

■ ■ ■

Yogurty's Collateral

"Yogurty's is a new self-serve frozen yogurt concept launching in Canada. As North Americans have become increasing health conscious, Yogurty's provides a guilt-free, healthy indulgence that is targeted to families. Jump endeavored to create a logo with classic styling that would also be at home in a modern, eclectic environment. We commissioned several illustrations that convey the exciting possibilities that come out of the product customization. These illustrations are used throughout a wide range of signage, packaging, collateral, and on the website." —JH

■ FIRM **Jump Branding & Design**, Toronto, ON, Canada
■ CREATIVE TEAM **Jason Hemsworth**, **Eric Boulden**, **Richard Patmore**, **Andrew Vysick**
■ CLIENT **Yogurty's**

■ ■ ■

Why? Poster

"Why? is a weird band that makes weird music. There is something about their odd approach to chopping up disparate music genres alongside stream-of-consciousness lyrics that always makes us think of a broken prism. Pink Floyd be damned." —EN

■ FIRM **Doe Eyed**, Lincoln, NE, USA
■ CREATIVE TEAM **Eric Nyffeler**
■ CLIENT **Why?**

■ ■ ■

You're a Good Man Charlie Brown Poster

"This was one of my favorite things I did in 2010, because it's so simple. In the show, some kids find a bunch of old Peanuts strips and act them out—the Charlie Brown character decorates his shirt with duct tape." —SH

■ FIRM **Hazen Creative, Inc.**, Chicago, IL, USA
■ CREATIVE TEAM **Shawn Hazen**
■ CLIENT **Northwestern University**

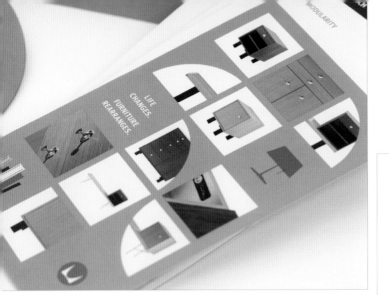

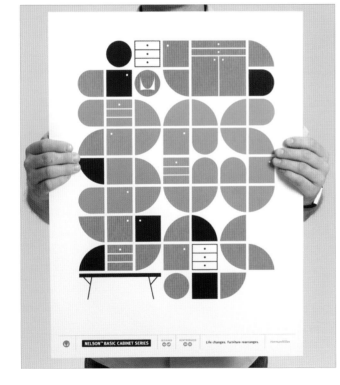

■ ■ ■

Herman Miller:
Nelson Basic Cabinet Series Campaign

"This project was a branding campaign for the reissue of the 1947 Nelson Basic Cabinet Series including a brochure, silkscreened poster series, and promotional video. I created the 'Life Changes, Furniture Rearranges' theme to express BCS's multifunctional, modular, and timeless design. This project was a turning point for me as a designer. Not only was it a chance of a lifetime to design for such an iconic product and company, but it marked the first time that a creative vision of mine was allowed to come to full fruition. I still look at this campaign, particularly these posters, and get a warm feeling inside." —*MK*

■ FIRM **Tandem Design**, Traverse City, MI, USA
■ CREATIVE TEAM **Maria Kinney**, **Jennifer Lake**, **Eric Daigh**, **Terence Mahone**
■ CLIENT **Herman Miller**

Facebook Holiday Gift

"The Facebook Holiday Gift is something we send out each year to some of our friends and clients as a small way of saying thank you. In 2009 we decided to try and make a gift that felt more unique and personal. Each recipient was given a custom wooden token that was redeemable online through DonorsChoose.org or Kiva.org for the cause of their choice. Additionally, each recipient received a Facebook themed art print." —*BB*

■ FIRM **Facebook**, Palo Alto, CA, USA
■ CREATIVE TEAM **Ben Barry**
■ CLIENT **Self-Promotion**

AIGA Philadelphia Design Awards Catalog

"This project is a catalog design for the AIGA Philadelphia Design Competition. The catalog print-run was limited to the same number of copies as the number of entries received (576), to represent all the work of the design community. Using a variable printing program, each cover is a different color on a predetermined spectrum—each one was a slightly different shade of color from the last, following the color scheme of ROYGBIV; making each catalog entirely unique—no two are alike." —*AE*

■ FIRM **gdloft, PHL**, Philadelphia, PA, USA
■ CREATIVE TEAM **Allan Espiritu, Mike Sung Park, Christian Mortlock, Matt Bednarik**
■ CLIENT **AIGA Philadelphia**

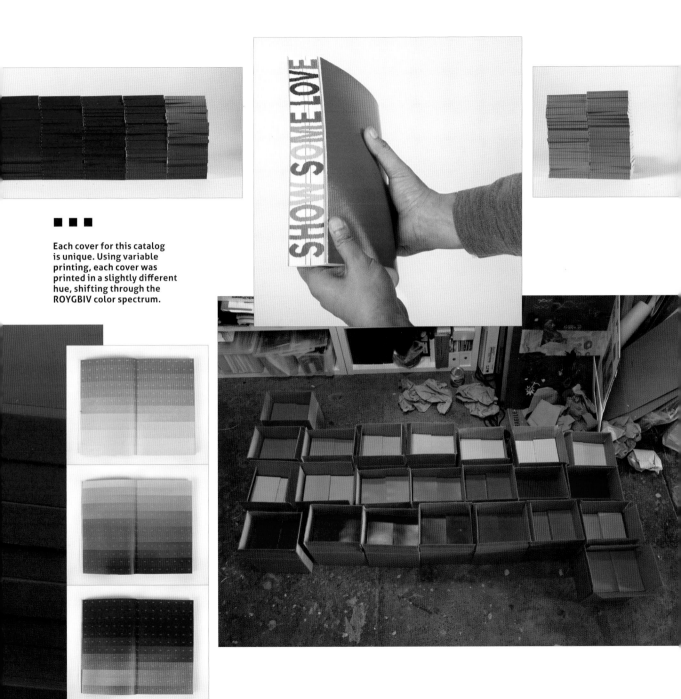

Each cover for this catalog is unique. Using variable printing, each cover was printed in a slightly different hue, shifting through the ROYGBIV color spectrum.

■ ■ ■

Waste Less

"This project began with an AIGA screenprinting workshop I attended soon after Earth Day. I collected litter in my neighborhood, and cut it up into 4"x6" cards, making collaged cards from all the interesting trash I'd collected. I screenprinted my WASTE LESS artwork on them, and purposefully misaligned the registration for added effect. The back of the postcard contained the message 'Every day is Earth Day.' I love how this project evolved organically and began with the act of cleaning up my neighborhood. I even got some new projects because of it!" —JDC

■ FIRM **Jenn David Design**, San Diego, CA, USA
■ CREATIVE TEAM **Jenn David Connolly**
■ CLIENT **Self-Promotion**

■ ■ ■

Los Angeles Public Library Children's Reading Program "Spy Books"

"Each summer, the Library Foundation of Los Angeles sponsors a Children's Reading Program for the city's local branches. The client provides us with the title of the program and we design the activities, as well as a folder, bookmark, book bag, and certificate. Our first execution of the theme was based on a vintage detective's case folder with illustrations appealing to kids. The client wanted a different approach, and asked for a James Bond/Mission Impossible-styled design. The games in the folder included deciphering various codes, spelling out a secret message with their answers. We also included a match game using the library's Dewey Decimal System." —GR

CUTTING
ROOM
FLOOR

■ FIRM **Epos, Inc.**, Hermosa Beach, CA, USA
■ CREATIVE TEAM **Gabrielle Raumberger**, **Brandon Fall**
■ CLIENT **Library Foundation of Los Angeles**

■ ■

The success of our design was measured by the fact that by the time the book was done, everyone at Grip was dying to sign up for Fall term.

■ ■

ENVIRONMENT

preserving, sharing, and extending human knowledge

163

■ **SAIC Admissions Catalog**

■ "When we found out we would be doing the graduate
■ viewbook for the School of the Art Institute of Chicago, we
definitely pinched ourselves. This is one of those dream projects where the subject matter was inspiring, the design was conceptually driven, and the client maintained the integrity of our concept. From the impressive presence created by the physical size of the book to its purple painted edges and minimalist cover design, we saw the opportunity for SAIC to stand out amongst other graduate viewbooks by creating a 'book as art object.' We sought to not only effectively educate, inspire, and convert potential students, but also to create a beautiful book in itself that embodied the multi-dimensional art-making process and conceptually-driven thinking of SAIC students." —*JB*

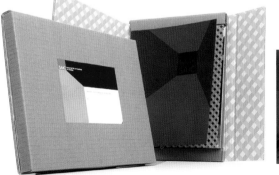

Chicago's Cultural Institutions

■ FIRM **Grip Design**, Chicago, IL, USA
■ CREATIVE TEAM **Joshua Blaylock**, **Camay Ho**, **Kelly Kaminski**, **Kevin McConkey**
■ CLIENT **School of the Art Institute of Chicago**

"Wash Me" 10 MINI. 10 Artists.

∙∙

- FIRM **Nico Ammann**, Zurich, Switzerland
- CREATIVE TEAM **Nico Ammann**, **Oliver Aeschlimann**
- CLIENT **BMW AG, MINI Switzerland**

■ ■

Great things in advertising and design are created when the client and the designer trust each other, and work together.

■ ■

Nico Ammann,
*Creative Director,
Nico Ammann Art
Direction & Design*

■ **What was the genesis of this project?**
■ *Nico Ammann:* Oliver Aeschlimann, former
■ PR Manager for BMW and MINI Switzerland
came to me with the idea to create a piece of art for MINI's 50th anniversary. We wanted to create something unique and inspiring, that comes from the heart of the brand MINI — and that's how we came up with the idea to create the book *Wash Me*.

How did the book concept come about?
NA: The idea for the book was inspired by the simple act of drawing or scribbling on a dirty car: Most people have written "Wash Me" at least once on a dirty car hood. So, we had ten artists each turn a MINI into their piece of art by cleaning and smearing paint off and on the car. *Art on Art.* Of course, the cover of the book is 'washable' too: With a sponge, you can wipe the title off the plastic cover.

It started as a small project for MINI Switzerland. Mainly, they wanted to use the book as a giveaway at car dealerships and trade shows. Then, several major newspapers gave it full page coverage. Then the book was communicated worldwide on BMW Group's Press Club. In the end, it reached people

all around the world through hundreds of websites from Germany, over Russia, and all the way to China. So, MINI not only got a book giveaway for tradeshows and dealerships, they also received a huge amount of worldwide publicity.

Fortunately there was no particular business goal behind this project, but the strategic goals were to create a product that would serve as a brand shaper, while also getting us media coverage. We couldn't imagine that the book would turn out so successfully and gain such global attention.

What was your favorite part of this project?
NA: We were able to develop our project without any constraints. We had this great understanding: the book had to be an authentic, candid involvement and collaboration with the artists, because that's the only way (and the only accurate way) to reach all the insider types—designers, artists, musicians, etc.—so that they'll create buzz around the work we've created.

It proves that great things in advertising and design are created when the client and the

designer trust each other, and work together. And of course, it was great to see how many people love the book, and the idea of it.

What was the most challenging aspect of the project?
NA: The budget wasn't much bigger than what MINI would spend on a few single page ads in a larger Swiss newspaper. This limited us, but also inspired our creativity.

If you would, let us in on a couple of interesting stories behind this project.
NA: At the end of the day, when the piece of art was created and photographed, we always ended up in a different car wash to clean the car again. You should have seen the people's faces there!

Why did you choose to do this as a print piece, rather than online?
NA: Every media has its advantages and disadvantages. I guess print (a book) still speaks to people, because it's something you can hold on to, something you can keep. On the other hand, without the Internet, we wouldn't have received the attention we did with this project. ■

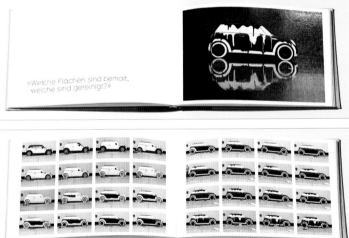

«Welche Flächen sind bemalt, welche sind gereinigt?»

■ For this MINI project, the creative team had
■ unprecedented freedom to build an artistic
■ collaboration that also served as a powerful
■ brand initiative for the auto makers.

■ ■ ■

The Preserve Campaign

"This campaign for The Preserve, a residential building built on the site of a former hot-sauce factory in New Orleans, is my favorite for two reasons: 1—Tons of type! We had blast exploring different type styles that truly gave that New Orleans feeling. Post-Katrina, New Orleans pride ran high, and people wanted to preserve their local flavor. 2—The research. To get into the right mindset, we took a trip down south to experience the city's culture and cuisine! We ate many po-boys in preparation for this project, inspiring us to create The Preserve hot sauce bottle—a fun, creative marketing tool, which was given out to prospective tenants." —LM

■ FIRM **Square Feet Design**, New York, NY, USA
■ CREATIVE TEAM **Lauren Marwil**, **Marcella Kovac**, **Michelle Snyder**
■ CLIENT **Domain Companies**

■ ■ ■

Anything But Typical

"Working on this project with Lizzy Bromley from Simon & Schuster was a delight. Having previously worked on some more technical projects that dealt with autism, it was exciting to approach it with a purely visual project. To capture the obsession, whimsy, and dislocation of an autistic boy's experience was a challenge. We made the cover very striking with simple coloring around obsessional linework, and utilized handwritten type which we peppered throughout the book's layout. Wrapping the whimsical thoughts of the abstracted boy around the cover provided a step into the protagonist's thought patterns and experience. I do love visualizing the mind and its processes in this literal mess of abstract patterns." —JGH

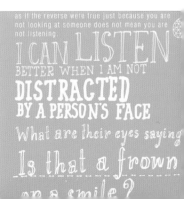

■ FIRM **James Gulliver Hancock**, New York, NY, USA
■ CREATIVE TEAM **James Gulliver Hancock**, **Lizzy Bromley**
■ CLIENT **Simon & Schuster**

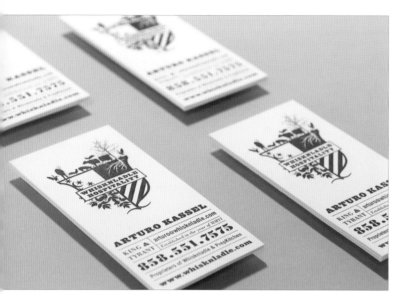

Whisknladle Hospitality

"The Whisknladle Hospitality logo and business cards were developed as an umbrella brand for the proprietors of Whisknladle and PrepKitchen. Their restaurants focus on the process of gathering local, seasonally-inspired ingredients, and preparing them in a simple and honest manner to offer a place where food and community come together. The executions of the brand reflect their rustic and historical inspiration." —BN

- FIRM **Bex Brands**, San Diego, CA, USA
- CREATIVE TEAM **Becky Nelson**
- CLIENT **Whisknladle**

CUTTING
ROOM
FLOOR

I'd listen to the band's music, think about their name, and try to put my first instinctual idea on paper

The Ottobar Posters

"While living in Baltimore, I designed a series of posters for a local venue, The Ottobar. Each week I was assigned one concert and I would have pretty much free reign to design a poster. I'd listen to the band's music, think about their name, and try to put my first instinctual idea on paper. This meant that sometimes the poster design was outside the realm of the usual imagery the band would use to present itself, but in my opinion, that is much more exciting and interesting." —AB

- FIRM **Ana Benaroya**, Jersey City, NJ, USA
- CREATIVE TEAM **Ana Benaroya**, **Craig Boarman**, **Whitney Sherman**
- CLIENT **The Ottobar**

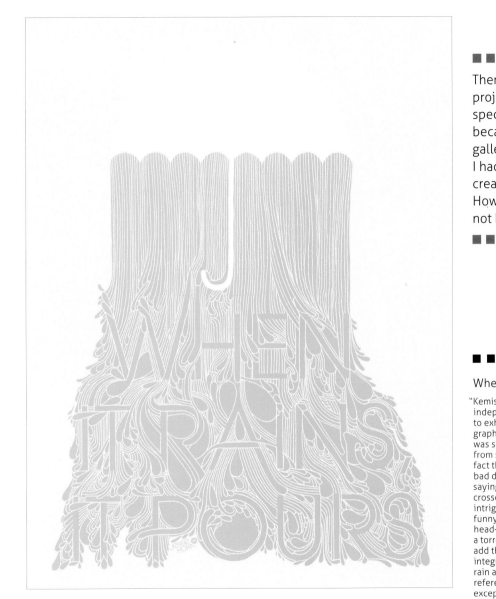

There wasn't a project brief or any specs to adhere to—because it was for a gallery show—I had complete creative freedom. How could I not have fun?

WhenItRainstItPours

"Kemistry Gallery is an independent gallery dedicated to exhibiting outstanding graphic design. This project was so fun because it started from such a simple idea—the fact that I was having a really bad day. From there the old saying 'when it rains it pours' crossed my mind, a funny yet intriguing concept. An equally funny visual popped into my head—'an umbrella within a torrential downpour.' To add the intriguing aspect, I integrated the lettering into the rain and boom (get the storm reference?)—I was done. Well, except for the hours of drawing and screen-printing. The result was a beautiful and intricate one color silkscreen printed on 100lb kraft Speckletone stock. The print measures 19"x25" and is signed and numbered in an edition of 15." —JH

■ FIRM **MAKE.**, Chicago, IL, USA
■ CREATIVE TEAM **Jesse Hora**
■ CLIENT **Kemistry Gallery**

44th Kent State Folk Festival Posters

"The big idea to 'unplug from technology, experience live music' was developed quickly and naturally. Both the copywriter and I love music. The idea grew out of bad concert etiquette we had witnessed—people ignoring the music to talk on the phone, or capturing grainy mobile phone video and pictures rather than focusing on the music. The first round of designs were inspired by country western concert posters and contained an eclectic mix of typefaces. It became clear that this didn't work, because the headlines were difficult to read. As a designer, I decided to simplify and not let the art direction get in the way of communication. By restricting myself to one font, the headlines really became the focus." —RW

- ■ FIRM **Marcus Thomas LLC**, Warrensville Heights, OH, USA
- ■ CREATIVE TEAM **Ryan Wolfe**, **Kevin Delsanter**, **Joanne Kim**
- ■ CLIENT **WKSU 89.7**

The commissioned illustrations helped to project the personality of the festival to a wider audience.

The Big Chill Campaign

"The Big Chill is made up of various music festivals, a record label—and even a bar. We needed a device to unite the different elements of the brand, so 32 illustrators were commissioned to illustrate the many facets of the festival and these were used on all marketing materials, including ticketing. Overall, we created an identity for The Big Chill group, as well as this advertising campaign to promote the festival. As a result, sales increased for the first time in two years during the first quarter of the year and the illustrations helped to project the personality of the festival to a wider audience." —MDH

- FIRM **bleach**, London, UK
- CREATIVE TEAM **Matthew Darcy Hunt**, **David Puzey**
- CLIENT **The Big Chill Group**

Strangers In Paradise: The Works of Reverend Howard Finster

"This book is a catalog of the exhibit of the works of Howard Finster at the Krannert Art Museum. Finster was a folk artist with an eccentric outlook and approach that, at first, is off-putting. Our challenge was to make the 'first impression' a positive one that invites the viewer to take a serious look at the man and his life's work. We overcame this 'first impression' issue by creating a book with a richly textured cover showing Finster's work. We intended this to communicate to the viewer unequivocally that this man is perceived by the Krannert Art Museum to be an important artist." —*CN*

■ FIRM **Nivens Design**, Champaign, IL, USA
■ CREATIVE TEAM **Haley Ahlers**, **Chuck Nivens**
■ CLIENT **Krannert Art Museum**

I was a young man still in my pajamas at 11AM, trying my hardest to not sound like my office was in the kitchen of a small apartment.

■ FIRM **One Lucky Guitar, Inc.**, Fort Wayne, IN, USA
■ CREATIVE TEAM **Matt Kelley**, **Paige Strong**, **Nate Utesch**, **Jake Sauer**
■ CLIENT **Matilda Jane Clothing Co.**

Matilda Jane Clothing Co. Marketing

"We began working with Denise DeMarchis' clothing company, Matilda Jane, in 2004. When Denise called One Lucky Guitar, she was full of anxiety and trepidation—OMG, she was calling an *ad agency*! I was a young man still in my pajamas at 11AM, trying my hardest to not sound like my office was in the kitchen of a small apartment in Fort Wayne—especially because there was a *clothing company* on the line. Little did I know that Denise was calling from her utility room, where she was starting a clothing company in between life. We finally met, two lone rangers trying not to get lost. Seven years later, MJ is a worldwide success with 20+ employees, and OLG is a booming 10-person design and marketing boutique. And we still get butterflies calling each other." —*MK*

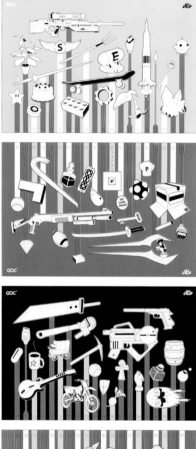

■ Game Developers Conference Posters

■ "For the 25th Game Developers Conference (GDC), show organizers
■ wanted a set of giveaways for attendees—something that
conference-goers could collect, trade, and interact with upon
registering for the weekend. Partnering with iam8bit Productions,
we designed a set of four posters filled with references from classic
and modern video games. Attendees were challenged to identify
each of the game items (without a cheat sheet), a kind of visual
scavenger hunt winding through 40 years of video game history.
The design and illustration had to transcend the styles and fads
that accompanied decades of video game iconography, from Atari
to Xbox 360, and we had a great time mining the treasure troves of
gaming for 80 unique items that made up the set of posters." —JA

■ FIRM **Hexanine**, Chicago, IL, USA
■ CREATIVE TEAM **Tim Lapetino, Jason Adam, Will Hobbs**
■ CLIENT **iam8bit Productions**

Table Nº1 Identity Materials

"Table Nº1 is Shanghai's first gastro-bar that serves up tapas-style modern European cuisine. The brand identity is based on the restaurant's focus on communal dining in a very simple and unpretentious environment, which explains the use of brown kraft & newsprint paper throughout the collateral system. Since the long communal tables in the restaurant are the central theme, the business card is designed to be a little table when folded up. Basic folders with clips are used for the menu. The distressed and rusted look of the clips is to align with its history at the location of this former warehouse. Order pads were created from newsprint papers that the staff can conveniently stamp the restaurant logo on." —YY

- FIRM **Foreign Policy Design Group**, Singapore
- CREATIVE TEAM **Yah-Leng Yu**, **Tianyu Isaiah Zheng**
- CLIENT **Table Nº1**

Misspent Poster

"This poster changed my life, literally. After receiving my MA from Kington University, I began looking for work in the UK. But it was the middle of a recession and jobs were scarce. I searched for eight months without success and was ready to return to my home country of Turkey. My plane tickets were ready. Right before I left, I spoke with Zoe Bather of Studio 8. She suggested I design a promotional poster and hand-deliver it to my favorite design studios. In one week, I had three job interviews and one job offer. This poster allowed me to stay in the UK, and I've also profited from selling copies as well." —EE

■ FIRM **Draught Associates Limited**, London, UK
■ CREATIVE TEAM **Ervin Esen**
■ CLIENT **Self-Promotion**

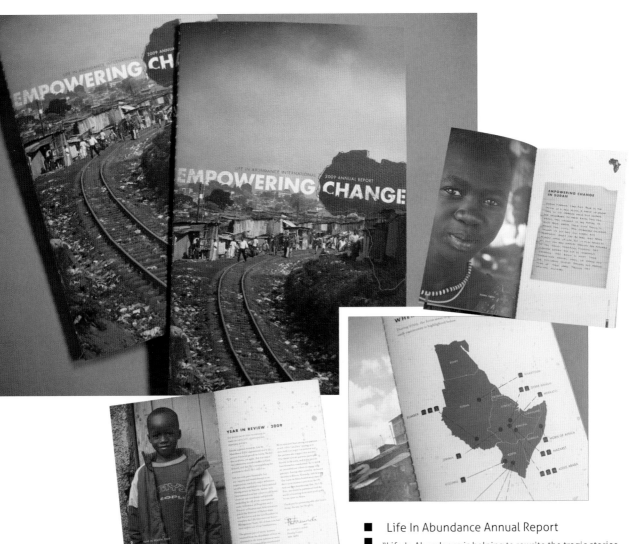

Life In Abundance Annual Report

"Life In Abundance is helping to rewrite the tragic stories that typically come out of Sub-Saharan Africa. Through this organization's work, new stories are emerging: communities learning how to take care of themselves; locals learning new skills; children attending new schools; micro-financing programs enabling individuals to start businesses and provide for their families; and communities gaining the resources to take care of each other and reduce the spread of an uneducated populace. Rule29 was able to help tell this story in the pages of an emotional and beautiful annual report that provided facts as well as tales of empowerment." —JA

- FIRM **Rule29**, Geneva, IL, USA
- CREATIVE TEAM **Justin Ahrens**, **Kerri Liu**, **Steve Czech**
- CLIENT **Life In Abundance**

Philadelphia Design Awards Mailer

"In order to promote the design community, AIGA Philadelphia developed their first regional design competition (PDA). Gdloft was asked to conceptualize, design, and oversee the copywriting of the 16-page call for entries brochure. Gdloft developed the concept 'show some love' to play off the acronym 'PDA'. The concept revolves around the idea that 'PDA' (Philadelphia Design Awards) can help build a sense of design community as well as become a motivating impetus (love) to creating good design work. The text is playfully made up of the top ten motivating phrases. In addition, as a metaphor for building community, the brochure can be deconstructed, and pieced together to reveal a poster." —AE

- FIRM **gdloft, PHL**, Philadelphia, PA, USA
- CREATIVE TEAM **Allan Espiritu**, **Mike Sung Park**, **Christian Mortlock**, **Matt Bednarik**
- CLIENT **AIGA Philadelphia**

■ ■ ■

Toormix New Papers Promo

"Toormix New Papers is a self-promotional editorial project containing a selection of projects developed at the studio from 2007 to the present. Originally, we were looking for a new way to show our portfolio, using a big format to display the projects. We contacted the press of a well-known newspaper to use its rotative press and paper. It was interesting using the same system as the mass newspapers! We also wanted an ephemeral product in the end, and this was perfect for that idea." —OA

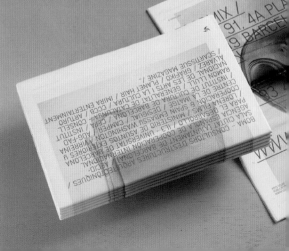

■ FIRM **Toormix**, Barcelona, Spain
■ CREATIVE TEAM **Oriol Armengou**, **Ferran Mitjans**
■ CLIENT **Toormix**

PACK
AGING

...

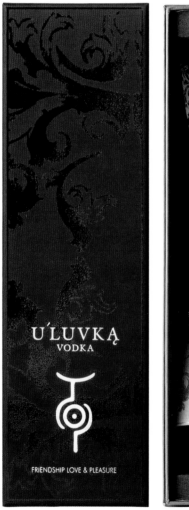

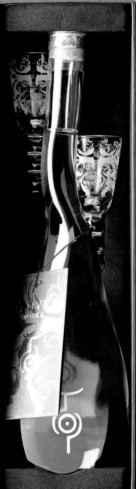

- FIRM **Aloof Design**, Lewes, East Sussex, UK
- CREATIVE TEAM **Sam Aloof**, **Andrew Scrase**, **Jon Hodkinson**
- CLIENT **U'Luvką Vodka**

U'Luvką Vodka

"We referenced illustrations and typefaces from 16th century Polish manuscripts to bring a sense of provenance and heritage to the brand. We also developed an innovative package to best display the bottle's silhouette. Since its launch, U'Luvką has redefined the luxury spirits category, winning more than 12 international packaging awards, and exceeding sales targets year after year." —JH

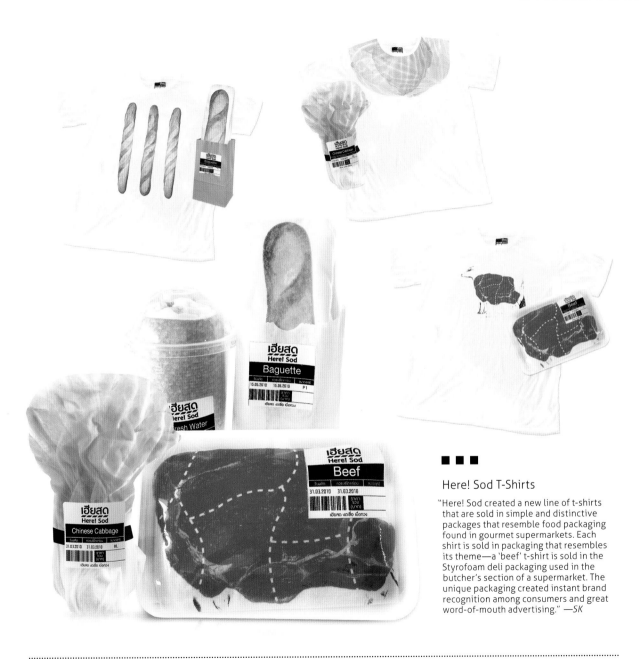

Here! Sod T-Shirts

"Here! Sod created a new line of t-shirts that are sold in simple and distinctive packages that resemble food packaging found in gourmet supermarkets. Each shirt is sold in packaging that resembles its theme—a 'beef' t-shirt is sold in the Styrofoam deli packaging used in the butcher's section of a supermarket. The unique packaging created instant brand recognition among consumers and great word-of-mouth advertising." —SK

■ FIRM **Prompt Design**, Bangkok, Thailand
■ CREATIVE TEAM **Somchana Kangwarnjit, Passorn Subcharoenpun, Chidchanok Laohawattanakul, Mathurada Bejrananda**
■ CLIENT **Here! Sod**

The whiskey is produced locally in the Hudson River Valley by Tuthilltown Spirits. They call it 'Four Grain Burbon.' We call it a life-saver.

Avec Holiday

"We felt inclined to inform our clients just how much they meant to us with this special New Year's gift. According to the Chinese Zodiac, 2011 is the Year of the Rabbit. 'Hare People' are known for their good taste and innovation. So we thought we'd say happy new year to our favorite clients with some tasty 'hare' of the dog. We asked them to join us in raising a glass and saying cheers to another year of tasty, innovative design. The whiskey is produced locally in the Hudson River Valley by Tuthilltown Spirits. They call it 'Four Grain Burbon.' We call it a life-saver." —CB

■ FIRM **Avec**, New York, NY, USA
■ CREATIVE TEAM **Camillia BenBassat**, **Gareth Geraty**
■ CLIENT **Self-Promotion**

■ ■ ■

Cunnington Specialty Cola

"The brief specified a unique, sophisticated label and custom PET bottle design for a new entry in the Argentine soft drink market. The objective was to differentiate the new beverage from the major players of the cola category. We were surprised when the CEO immediately fell in love with the most innovative design proposal we presented. He even refused to test the design with consumers, completely confident that the package would be a success. In record time, we delivered the label artwork and 3D files to manufacture the PET bottle molds. The product reached shelves 45 days after the initial concept presentation. The icing on the cake was winning a Silver Pentaward only a few months later!" —HB

■ FIRM **tridimage**, Buenos Aires, Argentina
■ CREATIVE TEAM **Hernán Braberman**, **Adriana Cortese**, **Virginia Gines**
■ CLIENT **Prodea**

High Roller

"High Roller is a new ultra-premium boutique Vodka brand created specifically for the Las Vegas market. The bottle's crystal cut design was influenced by the martini shakers and crystal decanters of the Rat Pack era and has the added bonus of making the bottle very easy to grip for fast-paced bar pouring in clubs. The top of the bottle has a notch that signifies a cut above the rest with the 'High' portion of the branding falling 'above the cut.' The final touch was developing an icon that would suggest both *Vegas* and *premium*. Our solution is a silver metal die, which reads both as an 'H' and a roll of seven, which will always be the 'High Roller' since six is the highest number found on dice." —DS

■ FIRM **CF Napa Brand Design**, Napa, CA, USA
■ CREATIVE TEAM **David Schuemann**, **Sara Golzari**, **Jeff Hester**
■ CLIENT **Souza Enterprises**

■ ■ ■

Annie's Naturals Salad Dressings

"Over a twenty-five-year history, Annie's line of all-natural and organic salad dressings has expanded to include more than 40 SKUs. DDW's brand redesign targeted evolving consumer lifestyles by enhancing the white space for shelf impact, unified the line with color-coding, and consistent logo treatment. Playful illustrations were developed with a homespun personality, to romance a particular aspect of each flavor." —BD

■ FIRM **Deutsch Design Works**, San Francisco, CA, USA
■ CREATIVE TEAM **Barry Deutsch**, **Kate Greene**, **Traci Merritt**, **Gina Triplett**
■ CLIENT **CPG Food**

■ ■ ■

Doves Farm Organic Cereals

"These packages were designed to communicate the healthy nature of the products without being too earnest. On the packaging for these new cereals we wanted to keep the illustrative tradition established on other cereals. Petra Borner, the illustrator, helped us to create two cereal packs that are slightly quirky and unusual and appeal to both adults and children." —RH

■ FIRM **Studio h**, London, UK
■ CREATIVE TEAM **Rob Hall**, **Petra Borner**
■ CLIENT **Doves Farm Organic Foods**

LEAP Organics Soap

"LEAP Organics is a bath and body products company out of Boston, MA. Moxie Sozo began working with founder, Luke Penney, when the company was in the initial concept stages. Faced with a highly competitive landscape, we identified four goals for developing the brand: 1) be bold; 2) be different; 3) take risks; 4) get noticed. Moxie Sozo worked with LEAP Organics to develop a personality that was appropriate, yet highly differentiated from other products in the category. Keeping within the spirit of the brand, the LEAP Organics' soap packaging was illustrated entirely by hand without the use of a computer". —LS

■ FIRM **Moxie Sozo**, Boulder, CO, USA
■ CREATIVE TEAM **Leif Steiner**, **Charles Bloom**
■ CLIENT **LEAP Organics**

YOLO Colorhouse

■ FIRM **YaM Brand**, Seattle, WA, USA
■ CREATIVE TEAM **Angela Mack**, **Michael Young**
■ CLIENT **YOLO Colorhouse**

■ ■

The founders are like-minded visual people who understand the importance of branding. We were fortunate they had the forethought to approach us during the research and development phase.

■ ■

Angela Mack,
Owner & Principal,
YaM Brand

■
■
■ **Tell us about your client.**
Angela Mack: Before starting YOLO Colorhouse, the founders' wall finishing company was a YaM Brand client. Working with paint every day presented them with a need for healthier paint and better color—the motivation behind the birth of YOLO Colorhouse. The founders are like-minded visual people who understand the importance of branding. We were fortunate they had the forethought to approach us during the research and development phase of the brand. Their concept of a premium, environmentally responsible paint line with select palettes was an idea we could immediately relate to. We considered ourselves the target market. And yes, every room of our home and studio is painted with YOLO Colorhouse paint.

Would you share your process with us?
AM: The environmentally responsible paint company required an identity reflecting the simple unity of art, nature, and science that are intrinsic to its line of paint. The stamp shape of the logo likens itself to a collaged stamp one may find in a scientist's field guide or an artist's sketchbook. The stamp was designed to be used in its simplest form as a logo, as well as extending the stamp to accommodate secondary brand elements, resulting in package design that attractively incorporates the logo. We introduced the single element of botanical illustrations as a secondary brand component to strengthen the unity of our message with art, nature, and science.

What is your favorite part of this project?
AM: The loyalty of our client made this one of our all-time favorite projects. YaM Brand was fortunate enough to have designed the initial logo and brand identity for YOLO Colorhouse when they started their environmentally responsible company.

This relationship of mutual trust has yielded packaging, retail displays, photography, advertising, a website, presentations, promotional items, cards, signage, display graphics, brochures, newsletters, and collateral—designed by people who truly understand their brand. We ensure that the soul and story of the brand is consistently ▶

YaM Brand worked with its client from the very beginning stages in R&D, through design and final production, yielding a unified vision for the YOLO Colorhouse product line.

■ ■

The people we work for have art backgrounds so they understand the visual language as well as the value of creative work. This is fantastic in that it eliminates much of the education process we have had to go through with other clients. How great is that?

■ ■

YaM Brand's involvement with YOLO Colorhouse has spanned hundreds of projects, from print to packaging and interactive work.

communicated across the board. We are completely invested in this brand and do what it takes to create the best possible products.

There have been just a few other times we've been lucky enough to create an identity from a company's inception, and then continue working to flesh out the brand identity through a variety of designed pieces. What sets YOLO Colorhouse apart is the sheer quantity and quality of projects we've had the opportunity to design over the last six years. YaM Brand has been involved in more than 300 projects with YOLO Colorhouse. Granted, some are quite simple (logo banners, business card reprints), but that's balanced by other intensive projects like the packaging, website, and editorial photography.

The people we work for have art backgrounds so they understand the visual language as well as the value of creative work. This is fantastic in that it eliminates much of the education process we have had to go through with other clients. How great is that? But it can also present its challenges. From the beginning we made sure we weren't just the "hands" that executed the client's ideas.

Being environmentally responsible is not only a value of our client, but a value of YaM Brand as a design studio. We specify FSC-certified printing with soy based inks on paper with at least some post-consumer recycled content whenever possible. ■

The White Company

"It's been an amazing opportunity to be involved in creating the look and feel for an entire retail environment, through designing each of the category ranges. The White Company, not surprisingly, uses minimum color in everything that it does, and our real challenge has been to create beautiful packaging for a huge array of different kinds of products with this restriction." —SA

■ FIRM **Aloof Design**, Lewes, East Sussex, UK
■ CREATIVE TEAM **Sam Aloof**, **Andrew Scrase**, **Jon Hodkinson**
■ CLIENT **The White Company**

Hansen's Natural and Diet Sodas

"Hansen's Natural and Diet sodas pioneered the natural soda category over 12 years ago by introducing premium sodas without caffeine, preservatives, artificial flavors, or colors. The redesign modernizes the product while maintaining existing equities for fruit illustration, logo, and colors. The new look is fun, natural, current and energetic." —BD

■ FIRM **Deutsch Design Works**, San Francisco, CA, USA
■ CREATIVE TEAM **Barry Deutsch**, **Harumi Kubo**
■ CLIENT **Hansen Beverage Company**

Fruta Del Diablo Salsa

"There is a wide variety of salsas in the marketplace, with offerings from small start-ups and international corporations alike vying for consumer dollars. Moxie Sozo wanted to create salsa packaging for Fruta Del Diablo that would distinguish it from everything else on the shelf and establish credibility for an unknown brand. By using hand-drawn illustrations inspired by the woodcuts of Mexican artist José Guadalupe Posada, we were able to lend authenticity to the salsa while reinforcing the product's heritage in traditional Mexican cuisine." —LS

■ FIRM **Moxie Sozo**, Boulder, CO, USA
■ CREATIVE TEAM **Leif Steiner**, **Nate Dyer**
■ CLIENT **Fruta Del Diablo**

Leatherback Candy

"Leatherback Printer wanted to promote a handful of new services and products, but do it a way that was different from methods they had used in the past. With summertime approaching, the idea of sending out nostalgic candy through a unique delivery system excited not only the sales team, but the owners as well—who were old enough to actually remember chomping on jaw-breakers, or sucking on Nik-L-Nips. The result is a fun, wacky, off-the-wall solution that brought in more business than the client could have possibly hoped for. It's funny how, when designers are actually allowed to do what they do best, everybody comes out a winner!" —KN

■ FIRM **Niedermeier Design**, Seattle, WA, USA
■ CREATIVE TEAM **Kurt Niedermeier**
■ CLIENT **Leatherback Printer**

■ ■ ■

Ciao Bella

"This project turned out to be a dream assignment. We were working with a client that couldn't afford photography and barely had a brief. They took on the challenge of trying to break into the gelato/sorbet category that already had strong existing brands. Ciao Bella was producing a successful, premium-line of products sold to the restaurant trade. The goal was to expand into retail—requiring a unique approach. We chose to produce a trendy line for them, focusing on color and graphics. Our challenge was to see if we could be successful without the support of photography. The result was instant success. " —SC

....

- ■ FIRM **Wallace Church, Inc.**, New York, NY, USA
- ■ CREATIVE TEAM **Stan Church**, **Nin Glaister**, **Jhomy Irrazaba**, **Jodi Lubrich**
- ■ CLIENT **Ciao Bella, Gelato Co., Inc.**

■ ■ ■

1792 Ridgemont Reserve Bourbon

"Barton brands, now Sazerac, asked us to create a name and design for their super premium eight-year-old bourbon. After many rounds of names we came to the conclusion they were not different enough. Instead of creating a brand name for them, we created a brand number: 1792. The number is significant as it is the year Kentucky became a state. The design is a very clean and simple one. We kept the bottle free from unnecessary graphic elements so as to allow the color of the spirit to be seen. We wrapped the neck with burlap to give the bottle a touch of 'down home' and create a tactile feel that was something natural. The new design is the cornerstone of the client's bourbon portfolio." —PD

....

- ■ FIRM **Di Donato Design**, Chicago, IL, USA
- ■ CREATIVE TEAM **Peter Didonato**, **Doug Miller**
- ■ CLIENT **Barton Brands**

Hummm

"A family package for the Hummm Ice Cream Store. 'There's this beautiful land where everything is sweet and the rain drops are made of ice cream, milkshake, coffee, and chocolate. Hummm.' Unfortunately at the end of the project process the client decided not to use the new design because of internal issues within the company." —JRM

- ■ FIRM **João Ricardo Machado**, Caldas da Rainha, Portugal
- ■ CREATIVE TEAM **João Ricardo Machado**
- ■ CLIENT **Hummm**

CUTTING ROOM FLOOR

IVI Classic

"We've been working for the IVI brand for more than 10 years. This project seemed like a great opportunity to say so much with so little. The bottle, supplied by the client, is based on the original shape of the first orangeade on the market—the one that made IVI famous and adored in the Greek market. The solution was obvious: less is more, with no label. The simple, authentic typographical style also communicates what we all love about IVI." —RS

- ■ FIRM **Red Design Consultants**, Athens, Greece
- ■ CREATIVE TEAM **Rodanthi Senduka, Gina Senduka, Angelopoulos Alexandros, Antonopoulos Giannis**
- ■ CLIENT **PepsiCo – IVI**

■ ■ ■

Organic Pet Superfood

"It's always satisfying to work with a client who is willing to zig while everyone else zags. The guys at Organic Pet Superfood were all about simplicity and color, which was a good match for my own design approach. They needed a new identity and packaging system that would better reflect the quality of their product, and their commitment to natural ingredients. In a marketplace dominated by dull, white, plastic bottles that look more like generic vitamins than premium pet nutrition, the simple, colorful design is positioned for the sophisticated, savvy pet owner. I love finding opportunities for style and personality within a limited set of design elements, and focusing on Garage Gothic and the interplay of black and bright colors gave us a really flexible foundation to use for the rest of the brand." —JH

■ FIRM **Barnhart**, Denver, CO, USA
■ CREATIVE TEAM **Jim Hargreaves**
■ CLIENT **Organic Pet Superfood**

Hammond's Candies

"Hammond's Candies is a Denver company that has been making candy with the same tempting recipes and same careful craftsmanship for 90 years. The previous packaging was simple gold and silver labels, often done in the factory. EBD worked with Hammond's for more than two years developing the logo, colors, and the language for the brand. The idea behind the concept was to establish a brand consistent with their 1920s heritage, and to reflect the continuation of their old-fashioned candy making traditions. We created a graphic system of color, logo, images, copywriting, and typography that all speak the Hammond's brand." —EB

- FIRM **Ellen Bruss Design**, Denver, CO, USA
- CREATIVE TEAM **Ellen Bruss**
- CLIENT **Hammond's Candies**

■ ■ ■

PUMA Clever Little Bag

"When Puma called us to rethink the shoe box, it was a simple question: what can be done differently with the shoe box? My thoughts were immediately about re-inventing the way shoes are shipped and how they are experienced by the consumer. Both the logistics and material research was really challenging, but we eventually found a way to reduce the materials and energy used to make boxes by 65 percent. The Puma Clever Little Bag delivers a better and long lasting experience, replaces the big plastic shopping bag at retail, *and* it is re-usable by the consumer past the purchase. One can either use the bag for travel, or find multiple re-uses in the home for storage and transport." —YB

■ FIRM **fuseproject**, San Francisco, CA, USA
■ CREATIVE TEAM **Yves Behar**, **Josh Morenstein**, **Nick Cronan**, **Seth Murray**
■ CLIENT **PUMA**

Corzo Tequila

"The Corzo team sought the IBC Design Group to design a sleeve that would amplify the product positioning in key markets. How do you go about enhancing a primary glass package which is altogether stunning? Well, why not drench it in a soft textured leatherette skin? We fabricated that skin in black to set off the exposed glass and blend beautifully with the cocoa brown and silver bottle graphic. We lined this beautiful piece with a soft leather velour so the bottle oozes into the sleeve for a tight luxe fit and feel. Done. Well-dressed. Dashing. Undeniably masculine." —NK

- FIRM **IBC Shell Packaging**, Lake Success, NY, USA
- CREATIVE TEAM **Norman Kay**, **John Varela**, **Jeri Newman**, **Christine Gao**
- CLIENT **Bacardi**

Seagram's Sweet Tea Vodka

"The tradition of enjoying a warm afternoon with friends on a covered porch while sipping a sweet Southern-style refreshment was the starting point for launching this new product line extension for Seagram's. We mixed retro style cues with urban textures for a smooth blend that captured market share across broad demographic segments." —JG

- FIRM **Deutsch Design Works**, San Francisco, CA, USA
- CREATIVE TEAM **Jess Giambroni**
- CLIENT **Infinium Spirits**

■ ■ ■

Death's Door Spirits

"Handcrafted from a small-batch copper still, Death's Door Gin and Vodka are perfectly suited for classic, pre-prohibition-style cocktails. Inspiration for the design was drawn from historical examples of perfume bottles and apothecary labels. Communicating the Death's Door story was also pivotal to the bottles' success. The spirits are crafted from wheat grown on Washington Island, Wisconsin, and Death's Door helps facilitate the island's return to sustainable farming practices." —JB

■ FIRM **Grip Design**, Chicago, IL, USA
■ CREATIVE TEAM **Joshua Blaylock, Molly Wells, Kelly Kaminski, Kevin McConkey**
■ CLIENT **Death's Door Spirits**

Tequila Malafe

"In general, tequila brands have very similar value offerings and identities. We call these tequilas 'Me Too' brands. Therefore, the challenge was to create a unique tequila brand that stands out from the crowded sea of 'Me Too' clones. We helped introduce differentiators like unique tequila flavors and contemporary designs, while targeting a sophisticated, cosmopolitan audience." —CG

■ FIRM **GaxDesign**, Guadalajara, Mexico
■ CREATIVE TEAM **Carlos Gaxiola**, **Jorge Aguilar**
■ CLIENT **Dibalva**

Tommyknocker Beer

"This was an exciting job for everyone at the agency, primarily because we are all craft beer fans. Another fun aspect of the creative process was touring the town of Idaho Springs, CO, where the Tommyknocker Brewery is. It's an old mining town, which provided a lot of visual inspiration. Some of the rustic storefronts inspired the hand drawn typography. I love creating design elements from scratch, especially with pen and paper, and the type turned out to have a lot of personality. And of course, the Tommyknocker character illustration we commissioned was especially fun to work on. We had to figure out how to make a mythical gnome look bad-ass, but still come across as a nice guy." —JH

CUTTING ROOM FLOOR

■ FIRM **Barnhart**, Denver, CO, USA
■ CREATIVE TEAM **Jim Hargreaves**, **Von Glitschka**, **Aaron Nava**
■ CLIENT **Tommyknocker**

One Village Coffee

- FIRM **Able Design**, Philadelphia, PA, USA
- CREATIVE TEAM **Greg Ash**, **Rob Franks**
- CLIENT **One Village Coffee**

■ ■

We wanted the design of the bag to reflect the personality of our business and team: approachable, dynamic, and fun. It was an important step that allows our brand to continue and grow with our company.

■ ■

Aaron Peazzoni,
General Manager, OVC

Tell us a bit about your client's story.
Greg Ash: One Village Coffee (OVC) is a specialty roaster located outside Philadelphia. They got their start wanting to reinvent the nonprofit business model by starting a for-profit business to fund humanitarian projects around the world. The CEO and startup team had a lot of energy and quickly grew a community of followers by spending more time than the competition doing demos and tastings. The whole premise behind "One Village" is an open invitation for people to come together. We recognize the power of the masses and as we used to say as kids, "two is more fun than one."

How did you approach this project?
GA: As the company grew so did the interpretation of who they were. OVC realized that something needed to be done to make their story more cohesive. This started by defining the term *village*. At Able, we started by interviewing coffee shop owners, wholesale purchasers, and everyday drinkers. We discovered a lot of different interpretations of the name from "a village in Africa supported by OVC" to "a village development program in which the proceeds supported projects around the world." These responses drove a lot of our conversation, so when each different group was asked why

they purchased OVC we were surprised at the common response that "the coffee is really good and the guys at OVC are good people."

We spent a couple days riding along with the sales team and watched them interact with coffee shop owners. They were greeted like friends, not vendors. They sat and drank espresso and talked business, coffee, and even family. We watched them hang with the crew at the Whole Foods as if they had been friends since grade school. It was remarkable. At the end of those interactions we realized that the word *village* is just another word for relationship—friend, cousin, homey, click, fraternity, club. One Village Coffee is about relationships with people.

Where did these insights lead your team?
GA: We needed the bag to feel like a village. We wanted it to be entertaining, capturing conversations in different ways. We looked at a lot of visual inspiration from movements by the masses—handmade signs, petitions, and murals. Interestingly many of the small coffee shops that serve One Village Coffee have some similar aesthetics—handwritten chalkboards, window signs, and DIY indie flyers on the bulletin board. The OVC bag needed to feel genuine and true. If it worked it might even feel like a movement. ▶

> We looked at a lot of visual inspiration from movements by the masses—handmade signs, petitions, and murals.

Greg Ash,
Principal, Able Design

Able Design sought to capture the qualities of conversation, interaction, and genuine humanity in its designs for One Village Coffee.

■ ■ ■

Able Design worked hard to help craft a cohesive brand story for One Village Coffee that would drive all design decisions moving forward.

What were OVC's business goals for this?

GA: OVC recognized that much of their success was due to the number of on-site demos they performed. As effective as on-site demos can be they are time consuming and require a lot of manpower. This project started with a desire for OVC to increase shelf presence at Whole Foods and other specialty grocery stores while decreasing on-site demos.

What was your favorite part of this project?

GA: I loved seeing the effects of the new packaging. Not only is the coffee selling better than before, but people are having conversations that start with the bag. People are asking questions. That's really cool to hear.

Why does this entry stand out from other work you've done?

GA: Like most of the work we create at Able, there is more to this bag than just packaging—if you want to find it. OVC has such a great mission, and knowing that helping their company grow is indirectly helping spread their humanitarian mission around the world feels pretty good. And every time I'm in Whole Foods with my four-year-old son he tells everyone that his Dad made that coffee bag. That's pretty cool.

Were there any specific point-of-purchase or shelf appeal concerns specific to this project? Was there anything unique about the audience for this project?

GA: Prior to this bag the OVC packaging had been mostly a maroon color. Making the shift to maroon and blue was a difficult decision. There were a lot of unknowns including whether or not customers would recognize the new brand. The new bag needed a more youthful and recognizable shelf presence, and the new design allows OVC to transition out of the local craft roaster, into a regional specialty roaster category. ■

Danone Yogurt

"Packaging is an interesting field. It's not only design and color, it's also shape, texture, visual graphics, ergonomics, ecology, and usability. It's a history of the product. For this project, I tried creating something simple, clean, laconic, and eye-catching for the retail shelf. There is minimal text and the shape combines ergonomics and usability. My favorite part is the 'op-art effect' and photo-realistic images." —IK

- FIRM **Freelance**, Klaipeda, Lithuania
- CREATIVE TEAM **Ilja Klemencov**
- CLIENT **3K**

Sprint Reclaim

"DDW spearheaded an initiative with Sprint to adopt a sustainability strategy for packaging design. We developed eco-friendly structural options covering multiple possible 'shades of green' for extensive consumer testing. The Reclaim package complements the more sustainable phone (made from 80 percent recyclable materials) and makes the total package even friendlier. The outer packaging and the phone tray inside the box are made from 70 percent recycled materials. All printing on the box, as well as the warranty information, are printed with soy-based ink. The typical thick-paper user manual has been replaced with a virtual manual that users can access online." —EK

- FIRM **Deutsch Design Works**, San Francisco, CA, USA
- CREATIVE TEAM **Erika Krieger**, **Pauline Au**, **Karl Bakker**
- CLIENT **Sprint**

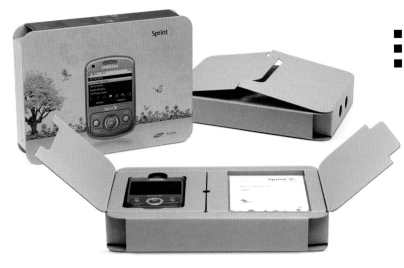

■ Nat-2 X Transformers

■
■ "This packaging was created especially for the Transformers Special Edition Nat-2 Stack 4-in-1 shoe, one style for each main TF character (Bumblebee, Optimus Prime, and Megatron). The collection launched in summer 2011, celebrating the release of the movie *Transformers 3: Dark of the Moon*. Each shoe comes with three different, interchangeable uppers which lets the shoes actually transform. Owning two pairs of the same size lets you mix and create your own combinations. In order to create a mysterious impression, we used raw pencil drawings of the Autobots and the Decepticon logo to contrast to the full colored shoes. The box is transparent, so once you place the shoes inside, the black and white figurines take on their own familiar, colored backgrounds." —*ST*

■ FIRM **K&T GmbH**, Garching-Hochbrueck, Bavaria, Germany
■ CREATIVE TEAM **Sebastian Thies, Matthias Thies**
■ CLIENT **Nat-2**

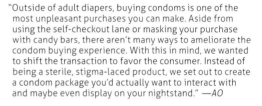

■ Sir Richard's Condom Company

■
■ "Outside of adult diapers, buying condoms is one of the most unpleasant purchases you can make. Aside from using the self-checkout lane or masking your purchase with candy bars, there aren't many ways to ameliorate the condom buying experience. With this in mind, we wanted to shift the transaction to favor the consumer. Instead of being a sterile, stigma-laced product, we set out to create a condom package you'd actually want to interact with and maybe even display on your nightstand." —AO

SIR RICHARD'S CONDOM COMPANY
12 ULTRA THIN
LUBRICATED WITH RECEPTACLE TIP

Latex condoms are intended to prevent pregnancy HIV/AIDS and many other sexually transmitted infections. When used correctly every time you have sex, latex condoms greatly reduce the risk of unintended pregnancy and infection though they cannot eliminate risk. **CAUTION: This product contains natural rubber latex which may cause allergic reactions.**

SIR RICHARD'S
CONDOM COMPANY

■ FIRM **TDA_Boulder**, Boulder, CO, USA
■ CREATIVE TEAM **Thomas Dooley**, **Jonathan Schoenberg**, **Austin O'Connor**
■ CLIENT **Sir Richard's Condom Company**

■ ■ ■

EatPastry Cookie Dough

"Founded by two chefs, EatPastry hired Moxie Sozo to help position the brand in Whole Foods and other natural products stores. Through the combination of French and raw food cooking techniques, the company has redefined the concept of healthy desserts. EatPastry asked Moxie Sozo to create a strong personality that would help differentiate their brand from competitors in the refrigerated aisle of the grocery store. The Art Deco–influenced packaging was illustrated by hand in deference to the small-batch, gourmet nature of the product." —LS

■ FIRM **Moxie Sozo**, Boulder, CO, USA
■ CREATIVE TEAM **Leif Steiner, Charles Bloom**
■ CLIENT **EatPastry**

Instead of stuffing the shoes
with even more paper, the company
includes a pair of socks in one
and a reusable shoe bag in the other.

- FIRM **TDA_Boulder**, Boulder, CA, USA
- CREATIVE TEAM **Thomas Dooley**, **Jonathan Schoenberg**, **Matthew Ebbing**
- CLIENT **Newton Running**

■ Newton Running

"Newton Running, based in Boulder, CO, is striving to produce shoes that have a very low impact on the environment. The company also wanted to look at the way the shoes were packaged and explore an alternative to the conventional printed cardboard boxes. We worked with Newton to develop a new package that is less box and more carton. The new package is a molded design that uses 100 percent post-consumer recycled material. The shape of the carton fits the shoe, eliminating the need to pack it with tissue paper. Instead of stuffing the shoes with even more paper, the company includes a pair of socks in one and a reusable shoe bag in the other." —TD

Consumers were asked to guess the four
mixed flavors in this mysterious concoction,
for a chance to win their photo on a Jones bottle.

Jones Jumble Soda

"Superbig was asked to create limited edition
packaging for Jones Soda Co.'s summer
seasonal beverages. To give these bottles
a little summer flair, we created three
illustrations which captured the essence of
the season's favorite pastimes. In addition,
consumers were given the opportunity
to guess the four mixed flavors in this
mysterious concoction for a chance to
win their photo on a Jones bottle." —DS

■ FIRM **Superbig**, Seattle, WA, USA
■ CREATIVE TEAM **Rich Williams**, **Kevin Walsh**, **Devin Stewart**
■ CLIENT **Jones Soda Co.**

PACT Underwear

"PACT Underwear retail packaging is an extension of the values behind the brand itself. We designed one box for each sex that use identifying stickers and cardboard inserts to accommodate each different style, print and partnership. The boxes and stickers are made from 100 percent recycled and recyclable paper. The design is more than just sustainable—it is fun and uniquely PACT. The whimsical die-cut windows on the front expose the expressive prints and colors of the underwear. Inside, each pair of underwear is wrapped around a card that speaks to the specific partnership and organization it benefits. In designing such a simple solution, we ensured that as the brand changes and grows, the packaging system could grow with it." —YB

■ FIRM **fuseproject**, San Francisco, CA, USA
■ CREATIVE TEAM **Yves Behar**, **Sara Butorac**, **Gabe Lamb**
■ CLIENT **PACT**

Two Pianos

"Gorisek-Lazar's Two Pianos is one of the rare piano duos in Europe, playing an extraordinary mixture of contemporary classical and jazz music. The challenge in designing this CD sleeve was to get maximum visual output using basic graphic elements. We wanted to highlight their vibrating energy using a single thin line 'traveling' through the sleeve (dividing it into two triangles—two pianos) and expressing the amplitude of a common musical voyage." —VS

- FIRM **Studio 360**, Ljubljana, Slovenia
- CREATIVE TEAM **Vladan Srdic**
- CLIENT **RTV Slovenija**

Boyer's Coffee

"Denver-based Boyer's Coffee wanted to redesign their identity, which had remained the same since 1965. They wanted to emphasize the quality and freshness that made them a premier roaster and purveyor of fine coffee. We used rich browns and accents of gold to achieve a more sophisticated look. The decaffeinated bags are differentiated with pearl white bags. Both use the new Boyer's schoolhouse logo as a centerpiece and homage to the company's heritage and historic factory." —TD

- FIRM **TDA_Boulder**, Boulder, CO, USA
- CREATIVE TEAM **Thomas Dooley**, **Jonathan Schoenberg**, **Barrett Brynestad**
- CLIENT **Boyer's Coffee**

■ ■
■ ■

We leveraged the beer's deep carmel-brown coloring into a rich brand palette.

■ ■ ■

Budweiser American Ale

"When Anheuser-Busch decided to introduce a vintage American lager recipe from the 1940s they asked DDW to turn on the tap to deliver a robust brand story. We leveraged the beer's deep carmel-brown coloring into a rich brand palette accented with script lettering and watermarks to build a craft-heritage branding toolkit." —*MK*

■ FIRM **Deutsch Design Works**, San Francisco, CA, USA
■ CREATIVE TEAM **Mike Kunisaki**, **Ben Hsieh**, **Robert Hunt**
■ CLIENT **Anheuser-Busch**

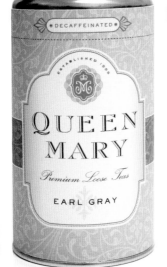

■ ■ ■

Queen Mary Tea

"I've never experienced more emotional ups and downs than I did with this project. Going in, I was made aware that the client had worked with two other designers, which is always a red flag. However, I convinced myself that the other participants weren't as persuasive nor as equipped to deal with difficult situations, so I charged ahead, hoping for the best. In the beginning, everything was great and I remember that first presentation like it was yesterday. The client literally started crying over the excitement she felt that someone had finally realized her vision. Sadly, I soon realized why the other creatives were let go, or likely quit. The client proceeded to manipulate, alter, and add until there was nothing left of the original design." —*KN*

■ FIRM **Niedermeier Design**, Seattle, WA, USA
■ CREATIVE TEAM **Kurt Niedermeier**
■ CLIENT **Queen Mary Tea**

CUTTING
ROOM
FLOOR

National Trust

"The National Trust charity looks after some of the UK's most important heritage buildings, priceless treasures, and land and has over 200 gift shops. Inspired by textile illustrations created by his seventeen-year-old daughter for a school art project, Rob Hall briefed and art directed his daughter to produce these lovely, freestyle fabric illustrations for National Trust's new packaging. The textile illustrations were loved immediately and, unusually, went through with no changes." —*RH*

■ FIRM **Studio h**, London, UK
■ CREATIVE TEAM **Rob Hall**, **Josie Hall**
■ CLIENT **National Trust**

Terrazas Wine

"The brief asked for a premium line of gift packs for the Argentine wine brand Terrazas, which are 'terraces' in Spanish. Inspired by the particular geography of the high elevation vineyards fed by the Andes meltwater, the packaging is adorned with graphic and structural effects signifying rocky terrain and flowing topography." —PI

■ FIRM **Pablo Iotti Design**, Buenos Aires, Argentina
■ CREATIVE TEAM **Pablo Iotti**
■ CLIENT **Terrazas Wine**

Emmi Swiss Yoghurt

- FIRM **Studio h**, London, UK
- CREATIVE TEAM **Rob Hall**, **Sarah Box**
- CLIENT **Emmi**

CUTTING
ROOM
FLOOR

When we presented
it became very
clear that our view
for Emmi in the UK
was not in line with
their European plan.
We remain firmly
convinced that it
was a major missed
opportunity.

Rob Hall,
Creative Partner, Studio h

How did this project come about?

Rob Hall: We'd been working with a Marketing Director of another Swiss dairy client for some years. The company was then sold and she joined Emmi Europe, the largest dairy company in Switzerland. Her main task was to launch an existing range of Emmi premium yogurts for children and adults aimed at the high end of the market into the UK.

What environment did the brand exist in?

RH: The majority of well-designed continental European yogurt brands tend to be more Scandinavian, French, and Spanish. The Swiss brands tend to lean toward the "cheesy," more old-fashioned style of communication. Yogurt packaging in the UK has been well established for many years and the marketplace (especially at the high end) is very sophisticated. Advertising plays a big part in creating consumer perception and "good for you" triggers. Simply having continental or Swiss dairy credentials is not going to impress, especially with an existing, tired old brand style, an anonymous brand that no one in the UK had heard of.

What was your firm's role?

RH: Our job was to create a unique Swiss yogurt brand in this competitive market.

It needed to stand alone and have huge impact to compete on shelf. The consumer doesn't want any more cheesy chocolate box mountains and blue sky Heidi stuff. Things need to appeal in a cooler way now, and that's the opportunity!

Through mood boards and research, we considered that it was best to proceed using fresh, clean, minimal design attributes—the graphic style Switzerland is famous for. The creation of the new Pure Swiss motif made sense, not only to communicate pure and cool expression, but also to act as an overall master brand and stable for other dairy products that would be launched in a similar way.

Could you share more about your concepts?

RH: Several concepts were presented but Emmi the cow was the overall winner. Emmi's Swiss heritage seemed to come to life when inhabited by the cow, a vehicle that could work on all levels from point-of-purchase, to advertising, to PR. In short, we felt it was an emotive and powerful way of announcing this new Swiss brand. Emmi the cow was a natural fit—totally alpine and drawn in a simple, flat style. She was fresh and contemporary, engaging and accessible for all ages, and an original way to show fruit differentiation. She had her

own personality, a good foil to everyone else's loud photography. We tweaked and developed Emmi until we felt she was the perfect cow! In 25 years of designing, she is one of our all time favorites.

Why did Emmi eventually get left on the cutting room floor?
RH: This kind of project (where you get a clean sheet to start with) is very rare in terms of brand design. For us, the exciting part was this: given the rather tired old ingredients we had to work with, we came up with a truly fresh and engaging brand proposition. Not only would it work for the packaging, but the designs would have also created a memorable and adaptable advertising platform perfect for everything, from posters to animation. We were very excited about it.

But sadly, when we presented to the Swiss board it became very clear that our view for Emmi in the UK was not in line with their European plan. While they understood and praised our reasoning, it was too big a step to take for just one of their many markets. Unfortunately, they were happy to carry on with what we might call the classic, fruity, milkmaid themes (albeit done to a good standard). We remain firmly convinced that it was a major missed opportunity. ■

■ ■ ■

Studio h sought to distinguish Emmi from other more established dairy brands in the UK marketplace, with fresh design and "the perfect cow" with personality.

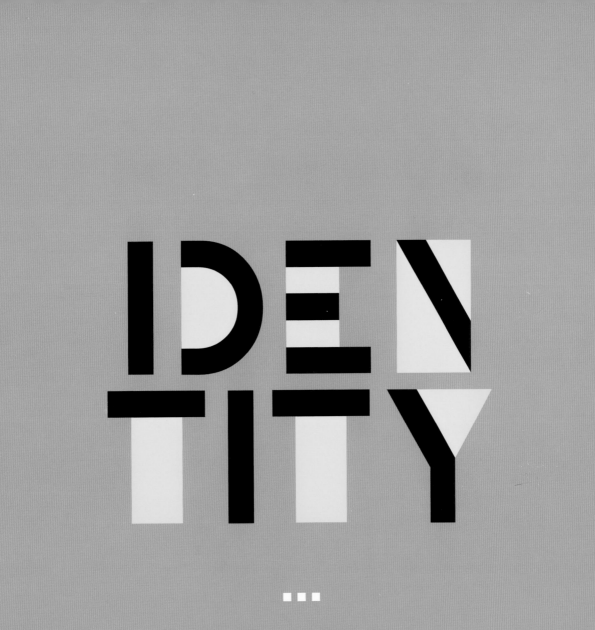

Bonk

- FIRM **Hazen Creative, Inc.**, Chicago, IL, USA
- CREATIVE TEAM **Shawn Hazen**
- CLIENT **Bonk**

Roots Remedies

- FIRM **YaM Brand**, Seattle, WA, USA
- CREATIVE TEAM **Angela Mack**, **Michael Young**
- CLIENT **Roots Remedies**

Anchor Marine

- FIRM **Webcore Design**, South Shields, Tyne & Wear, UK
- CREATIVE TEAM **Daniel Evans**
- CLIENT **Anchor Marine**

Titsa

- FIRM **Valladares Diseño y Comunicación**, Santa Cruz, Spain
- CREATIVE TEAM **José Jiménez Valladares**
- CLIENT **Titsa**

SEAMLUS

Seamlus Cloud Computing Systems

- FIRM **3 Advertising**, Albuquerque, NM, USA
- CREATIVE TEAM **Jesse Arneson**, **Sam Maclay**
- CLIENT **Seamlus Cloud Computing Systems**

Sound Machine

- FIRM **Kliment**, Sofia, Bulgaria
- CREATIVE TEAM **Kliment Kalchev**
- CLIENT **Sound Machine**

Tim

- FIRM **Tim Bjørn – Design Studio**, Copenhagen, Denmark
- CREATIVE TEAM **Tim Bjørn**
- CLIENT **Self-Promotion**

Myrtle Dove

- FIRM **Whitney Sherman Illustration**, Baltimore, MD, USA
- CREATIVE TEAM **Whitney Sherman**
- CLIENT **Myrtle Dove Vintage**

The business system utilizes a multi-use tape
featuring icons of things that are 'vital' to
the agency's staff, from beer to foosball.

■ Barnhart

■ "Barnhart is an advertising and design agency
■ in Denver, CO—recently rebranded as the
agency that drives their clients to 'Be Vital.'
The business system utilizes a multi-use tape
featuring icons of things that are 'vital' to
the agency's staff, from beer to foosball. A
new logo was also developed, inspired by
the agency's Art Deco surroundings." —JH

■ FIRM **Barnhart**, Denver, CO, USA
■ CREATIVE TEAM **Jim Hargreaves**
■ CLIENT **Self-Promotion**

Moderna

Diseño Argentino

CUTTING
ROOM
FLOOR

Hummm

- FIRM **João Ricardo Machado**, Caldas da Rainha, Portugal
- CREATIVE TEAM **João Ricardo Machado**
- CLIENT **Hummm**

Moderna

- FIRM **Pablo Iotti Design**, Buenos Aires, Argentina
- CREATIVE TEAM **Pablo Iotti**
- CLIENT **Manifesto**

yogen früz

Yogen Früz

- FIRM **Jump Branding & Design**, Toronto, ON, Canada
- CREATIVE TEAM **Jerry Alfieri**, **Jason Hemsworth**, **Eric Boulden**
- CLIENT **Yogen Früz**

Candysource

- FIRM **Hayes Image**, East Geelong, Victoria, Australia
- CREATIVE TEAM **Josh Hayes**
- CLIENT **Candysource**

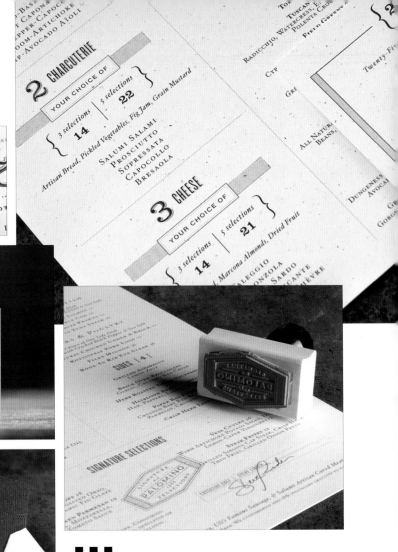

Palomino Restaurant

"Palomino has been a Seattle staple for 20 years. However, being a twenty-year-old company, and still wanting to remain relevant to a young audience, they decided it was time for a refresh and to expand past their current eight locations. We were given the opportunity to overhaul Palomino's brand across all consumer touch-points, including logo, menus, interior, advertising, website and messaging." —DS

■ FIRM **Superbig**, Seattle, WA, USA
■ CREATIVE TEAM **Kevin Walsh**, **Rich Williams**, **Matt Fagerness**, **Devin Stewart**
■ CLIENT **Restaurant's Unlimited**

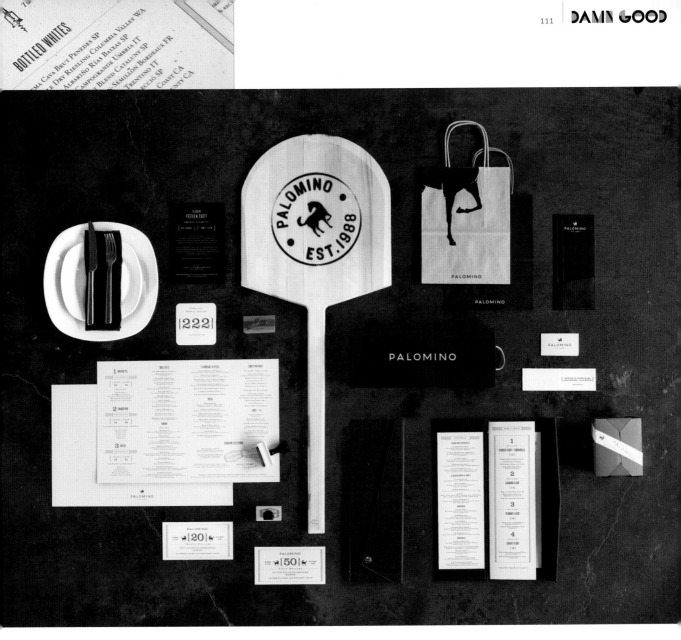

It was important for us to reflect the vibrance, heritage, and dedication to quality in Palomino's new identity system and to maintain consistency in all endeavors.

Korubo

- FIRM **Bencium**, Budapest, Hungary
- CREATIVE TEAM **Bence Csernak**
- CLIENT **Korubo**

LiQWd

- FIRM **UNIT design collective**, San Francisco, CA, USA
- CREATIVE TEAM **Ann Jordan**, **Shardul Kiri**
- CLIENT **Olatherapy**

Perkins Pickles

- FIRM **Studio Junglecat**, Chicago, IL, USA
- CREATIVE TEAM **Matthew Wizinsky**
- CLIENT **Perkins Pickles**

Tango Mango Italian Ice Co.

- FIRM **Studiofluid, Inc.**, Los Angeles, CA, USA
- CREATIVE TEAM **Ben Thompson**, **Bobby Dragulescu**, **Stuart Silverstein**
- CLIENT **Tango Mango Italian Ice Co.**

Players by the Sea

- FIRM **Brunet-García Advertising & PR**, Jacksonville, FL, USA
- CREATIVE TEAM **Jorge Brunet-García**, **Jefferson Rall**, **Aerien Kloske**, **Jenny Camet**
- CLIENT **Players by the Sea**

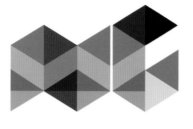

NEXT
GENERATION

YOUTH & FAMILY SERVICES

Next Generation

- FIRM **Erwin Hines**, San Diego, CA, USA
- CREATIVE TEAM **Erwin Hines**
- CLIENT **Next Generation**

New Day

- FIRM **3 Advertising**, Albuquerque, NM, USA
- CREATIVE TEAM **Jesse Arneson**, **Tim McGrath**
- CLIENT **New Day New Mexico**

wüstenrot

Wüstenrot

- FIRM **Designagentur Wagner**, Mainz, Germany
- CREATIVE TEAM **Oliver Andreas Wagner**
- CLIENT **Wüstenrot Bausparkasse AG**

■■ ■■

I was able to create the brand based
on some trademark New York details:
wrought iron railings, gold, and texture.

■■ ■■

■ Joanna Vargas
■
■ "The Joanna Vargas rebranding was one of our favorites
for multiple reasons. First, I love New York since I grew
up there and love the culture and metropolitan energy.
Also, given my personal history and that the salon is
on Fifth Avenue, I was able to create the brand based
on some trademark New York details: wrought iron
railings, gold, and texture. These were represented
in a very intricate embossing/debossing. I also used
my hand-lettering skills to create this custom pattern
which clients were hesitant to touch at first since the
materials looked so 'rich.' They quickly got over that
and now find any excuse to buy something, just to
walk out with one of the Joanna Vargas bags." —*DB*

....

■ FIRM **DBD International, Ltd**, Menomonie, WI, USA
■ CREATIVE TEAM **David Brier**
■ CLIENT **Joanna Vargas Salon**

CUTTING
ROOM
FLOOR

Get Grok

- FIRM **LifeBlue Media**, Allen, TX, USA
- CREATIVE TEAM **Ben Tautfest**
- CLIENT **Get Grok**

Battleship

- FIRM **Rickabaugh Graphics**, Gahanna, OH, USA
- CREATIVE TEAM **Eric Rickabaugh**, **Dave Cap**
- CLIENT **Hasbro, Inc.**

MCA Denver Heart Club

- FIRM **Ellen Bruss Design**, Denver, CO, USA
- CREATIVE TEAM **Ellen Bruss**
- CLIENT **Museum of Contemporary Art Denver**

Medicine in Motion

- FIRM **3 Advertising**, Albuquerque, NM, USA
- CREATIVE TEAM **Tim McGrath**, **Sam Maclay**
- CLIENT **Medicine in Motion**

■ Greenup Industries

■ "Greenup Industries is a record imprint and subscription service
■ offering seasonal batches of limited edition vinyl releases of
music in the freenoise, improv, and psych arenas. The identity
is designed to maintain its own sense of coherency while
encapsulating a broad range of audio possibilities. The logo
includes a custom work mark, which is equally geometric and
calligraphic—like 'calligraphy by machines.' The identity
references the sensibilities of psychedelia without focusing on any
particular period of time. Across business cards, T-shirts, buttons,
and stickers, this palette extends with basic geometric shapes
hand drawn over imperfect surfaces, thus extending the core
concept: a human touch via instruments and machines." —MW

■ FIRM **Studio Junglecat**, Chicago, IL, USA
■ CREATIVE TEAM **Matthew Wizinsky**
■ CLIENT **Greenup Industries**

DAVID

st and
wn for his
sitions
s, and
onds to
artist
ight
the SF
blend of
ic. Mason
e work of

Bay Area. Ochs, w
the soulful traditi
and sinawi impro
two musical style
improvisational ja
what he describes
ences that awake

JUANA MOLIN
THE CELLO CH
Sat, Aug 22, 8 pm,
$25 regular; $20
teacher, senior; $

Argentine singer
egorization. Her r
folk, ambient and
compared by criti
Lisa Germano. Th
originally rose to
Spanish-speaking

■ ■ ■

Yerba Buena Center For the Arts Summer 2009

"Frankly, it would be hard to not have fun with an arts
institution client that prides itself on bucking the status
quo. Both YBCA's executive director and director of
marketing were insightful, daring people who constantly
challenged us to do better work. We almost didn't
show the chosen idea in the initial design presentation
because we thought it was too wacky. That solution, with
its combination of subversion and whimsy, was very
unexpected coming from an established arts institution,
yet it captured YBCA's ethos perfectly. YBCA was also
one of the first arts institutions of its stature to champion
graffiti and street art, so we thought it appropriate to
commandeer this medium's methodology. It's one of the
rare projects where we were actually nervous about what
the reaction might be, since there was really no middle
ground in its communication and intent. People basically
loved the campaign or hated it. That ended up being the
most delightful part for us, because how often does any
design work really provoke a strong reaction?" —EH

■ FIRM **Volume Inc.**, San Francisco, CA, USA
■ CREATIVE TEAM **Eric Heiman**, **Adam Brodsley**, **Talin Wadsworth**, **Kim Cullen**
■ CLIENT **Yerba Buena Center for the Arts**

CHERIE SMITH JCCGV

JEWISH BOOK FESTIVAL

Tytology

- FIRM **Webcore Design**, South Shields, Tyne & Wear, UK
- CREATIVE TEAM **Daniel Evans**
- CLIENT **Tytology**

Jewish Book Festival

- FIRM **Seven25. Design & Typography**, Vancouver, BC, Canada
- CREATIVE TEAM **Isabelle Swiderski**, **Jaime Barrett**
- CLIENT **Cherie Smith Jewish Book Festival**

QFort

- FIRM **Brandient**, Bucharest, Romania
- CREATIVE TEAM **Cristian 'Kit' Paul**
- CLIENT **Casa Noastra Ltd.**

Tentación

- FIRM **HollyDickensDesign, Inc.**, Chicago, IL, USA
- CREATIVE TEAM **Holly Dickens**, **Claudia Boggio**
- CLIENT **Victoria**

Electrecords

- FIRM **Kliment**, Sofia, Bulgaria
- CREATIVE TEAM **Kliment Kalchev**
- CLIENT **Electrecords**

Household Ideas

- FIRM **Leibold Associates, Inc.**, Neenah, WI, USA
- CREATIVE TEAM **Joe Maas**
- CLIENT **Household Ideas**

Mesí Custom Gift Designs

- FIRM **Hexanine**, Chicago, IL, USA
- CREATIVE TEAM **Tim Lapetino**, **Jason Adam**
- CLIENT **Mesí Custom Gift Designs**

ITI

"ITI is a pioneer in automation technology, solving everyday challenges in all parts of life. The brand communication we developed for ITI is built upon the business idea itself. Appearing different on every surface, the visual expression is a representation of life, freedom, and possibilities. We established their core values and developed full visual identity program and slogan." —SH

FIRM **Heydays**, Oslo, Norway
CREATIVE TEAM **Stein Henrik Haugen**
CLIENT **ITI**

Nobis Interactive

■ FIRM **Erwin Hines II**, San Diego, CA, USA
■ CREATIVE TEAM **Erwin Hines II**
■ CLIENT **Nobis Interactive**

■ ■ ■

This redesign was the first project I was given and was a big reason why I was chosen to come on and help rebrand this company.

■ ■

Erwin Hines II,
*Creative Director,
Nobis Interactive*

nobis

■ **How does the story of your client fold into**
■ **this project?**
■ *Erwin Hines II:* Nobis Interactive is a full-service digital agency based in San Diego. In the early years, Nobis mainly worked in the realm of online marketing and SEO. The former Nobis logo captured the spirit of the company at the time, but as their client list and professional expertise grew, it was clear that it no longer represented them well. Now, with three integrated service divisions (Nobis Interactive, Nobis Production, and Nobis Strategy) and a philanthropy arm (Nobis Aid) Nobis was looking for an identity system that not only reflected their present moment, but could grow and evolve with them. My first project as lead designer was to lead the redesign of the Nobis brand, which encompassed a new mark, website, stationary, and other corporate collateral.

How did your concept develop?
EH: Through all of our conversations about the Nobis mission, vision, and the general direction of the digital industry, one thing that really resonated with the team was the idea of "dare to do different"—a very bold and energetic statement that stayed with me as we moved through the process.

After months of research, brainstorming, and immersion in the Nobis environment, it became clear that the essence of the brand could be embodied in three simple words: evolution, experimentation, and innovation. We wanted to implement these in a bold and energetic way. A fluid and somewhat abstract "N" grew out of the concept organically, and its shape made it easy to apply the logo in a unique way to each of the developing Nobis divisions (Nobis Interactive, Nobis Production, Nobis Strategy, and Nobis Aid) while still maintaining continuity. We gave each department its own color palate/scheme and unique design within the "N."

We wanted to develop a mark that could be powerful with or without the logotype. After experimenting with other iterations, we wound up using the outline of the "N" as the shape for our business cards, printed with the appropriate matching divisional colors.

Tell us about the business goals you met along the way.
EH: The project goals were: refresh the look and feel of Nobis, reflect the emerging ▶

One thing that really resonated with the team
was the idea of "dare to do different"—
a very bold and energetic statement that stayed
with me as we moved through the process.

BEFORE   **AFTER**

My favorite part was finding a way to embody the essence of the Nobis brand visually and then watching it evolve with each new application.

structural changes and objectives of each division, and create a flexible mark that would work across multiple applications. The members of the Nobis team were excited about the new logo—we received plenty of compliments when we passed out our business cards.

What else can you tell us about Nobis?
EH: Initially, Nobis worked mostly in the realm of online marketing, and merged with an SEO agency in 2006 to order to offer a more comprehensive suite of services.

The previous logo, developed around the time of that merger, was able to capture the potential of this merger. However, as their client list and professional expertise grew, it was clear that Nobis too had grown—right out of their former logo, which is how this project originated.

The owner was really trying to transform the company into a fully integrated digital agency. Figuring out how to express that visually was very exciting. The fluid concept was the first thing that came to my mind and It started out as an origami shape—I was folding pieces of paper. I wanted it to fold up at first, but in the end, we moved away from that and used the "N" as a window that can display different things.

What was your favorite part of this project?
EH: Honestly, my favorite part was finding a way to embody the essence of the Nobis brand visually and then watching it evolve with each new application.

Why does this entry stand out from other work you've done?
EH: I've done websites and logos for other companies before, but this was my first time redesigning the branding of the company I

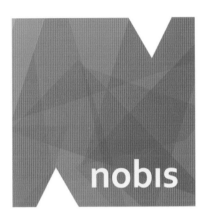

nobis

Kevin Lee Designer

p:	656.817.9812
e:	klee@nob.is
w:	www.nob.is

was working for. It really made a difference being just a stone's throw away from the CEO and other executives each day, throughout the whole process.

What was the most challenging aspect of designing this identity?

EH: Ironically, the most challenging part of this project was the very thing that set it apart from my other projects—I mean, since I work for the client, it's like I am the client. And like many designers, I am almost never 100 percent satisfied with my own personal branding. The challenge was creating something that I really loved.

Was there anything unique about the audience for this project?

EH: With this redesign, our goal was not only to grab the attention of forward-thinking clients, but also attract new team members who live on "the bleeding edge" in the digital realm.

What do you see as the advantages of print versus other media?

EH: I really like web design and app design, but the one thing that both lack is a certain tactile experience. Our experience with all digital media feels (physically) the same. I can be interacting with a beautiful website or app, but on my computer my finger is glued to the mouse or swiping across the screen on my tablet. You never really get to touch or feel any textures. With print, texture adds not only another layer of beauty and detail, but very real engagement with the medium. Personally, I have memories of books I've read based on the tactile experience alone.

With this in mind, we were very particular about the stock used for our business cards. We wanted enough weight so that the corners would be defined, and just the right amount of texture to subtly convey our quality and integrity.

How did you use the strengths of print?

EH: One of the most exciting aspects of this project was creating the cards. As I mentioned, we were particular about the stock that we used and we also used a custom die cut in the shape of the "N" mark to reinforce the flexibility of the mark. The mark became the card. ■

■ ■ ■

Designer Erwin Hines worked within Nobis Interactive to create a new identity that reflected the organization's changes in structure and mission.

Berg & Berg

"Founded by Karin and Mathias in 2009, Berg & Berg asked us to develop a full visual identity, including stationery, packaging and web shop. Striving to create products of the highest quality possible, their goal is that every product will become a trusted friend in your wardrobe: loved, cared for, and enjoyed for many years to come. Our work included business cards, hangtags, compliment slip, stickers, a web shop, and advice on packing the products." —SH

■ FIRM **Heydays**, Oslo, Norway
■ CREATIVE TEAM **Stein Henrik Haugen**
■ CLIENT **Berg & Berg**

Italian Festival in Liverpool Mexico

- FIRM **Factor Tres**, Mexico City, Mexico
- CREATIVE TEAM **Sergio Enriquez, Rodrigo Cordova, Angel Gonzalez, Malena Gutierrez**
- CLIENT **Liverpool Department Store**

Investment Banking Institute

- FIRM **Corse Design Factory**, Rego Park, NY, USA
- CREATIVE TEAM **Nigel Sielegar**
- CLIENT **Investment Banking Institute**

The Mysts of Time

- FIRM **Studio Junglecat**, Chicago, IL, USA
- CREATIVE TEAM **Matthew Wizinsky**
- CLIENT **The Mysts of Time**

Dixon's Apple Orchard

- FIRM **3 Advertising**, Albuquerque, NM, USA
- CREATIVE TEAM **Jesse Arneson, Jason Rohrer**
- CLIENT **Dixon's Apple Orchard**

Art Center Alumni Council

- FIRM **Gee + Chung Design**, San Francisco, CA, USA
- CREATIVE TEAM **Earl Gee**
- CLIENT **Art Center College of Design**

UTOPIA

- FIRM **Kliment**, Sofia, Bulgaria
- CREATIVE TEAM **Kliment Kalchev**
- CLIENT **Utopia DJ School**

It Takes A Team

- FIRM **m district**, Pasadena, CA, USA
- CREATIVE TEAM **Christian Morin**
- CLIENT **A Better LA**

The Dwell Home

- FIRM **Hazen Creative, Inc.**, Chicago, IL, USA
- CREATIVE TEAM **Shawn Hazen**
- CLIENT **Dwell Magazine**

Hooray Purée

"This is one of those projects where we were given creative control over practically every aspect of the brand, from the name of the product to the branding, positioning in the marketplace, packaging, website, photography, and marketing. The newness of Hooray Purée's concept and mission not only meant the design had to be inviting and engaging, but it also had to educate the consumer on what this product is and how it could be used. An integral part of the selling and educational tools was the food photography used on the recipe cards, in which we spearheaded a three-day shoot and discovered our new love and hidden talent for food styling." —JB

- FIRM **Grip Design**, Chicago, IL, USA
- CREATIVE TEAM **Joshua Blaylock**, **Camay Ho**, **Kelly Kaminski**, **Kevin McConkey**
- CLIENT **Hooray Purée**

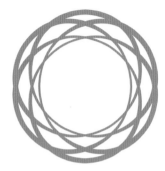

The Gutter

- FIRM **3 Advertising**, Albuquerque, NM, USA
- CREATIVE TEAM **Tim McGrath**, **Sam Maclay**
- CLIENT **The Gutter**

Pilates Pro

- FIRM **Hazen Creative, Inc.**, Chicago, IL, USA
- CREATIVE TEAM **Shawn Hazen**
- CLIENT **Pilates Pro / Pilates Professional Network Inc.**

Spain Arts & Culture

- FIRM **toormix**, Barcelona, Spain
- CREATIVE TEAM **Oriol Armengou**, **Ferran Mitjans**
- CLIENT **Embassy of Spain**, Washington DC

■ ■ ■

Pasadena Wine Festival

"Working with startups is something we always find rewarding. I personally love the process of shaping a fragile idea and helping it take flight. Our client came to us needing an identity and supporting collateral that would connect with three distinct audiences. Convincing advertisers, vendors and attendees they need to get on board is never an easy task, but as a first-time festival with no track record or previous ticket sales, the hurdle was significantly higher. We created a warm and vibrant identity that connects with a sophisticated, fun-loving audience, then extended it to press kits, website, tickets and signage. The festival was an overwhelming success in 2009 and is now an annual event." —BT

■ FIRM **Studiofluid, Inc.**, Los Angeles, CA, USA
■ CREATIVE TEAM **Ben Thompson, Estevan Benson**
■ CLIENT **Pasadena Wine Festival**

PROCESSED
IDENTITY

Yummy

- FIRM **João Ricardo Machado**, Caldas da Rainha, Portugal
- CREATIVE TEAM **João Ricardo Machado**
- CLIENT **Yummy Ice Cream**

Processed Identity

- FIRM **idApostle**, Ottawa, AL, Canada
- CREATIVE TEAM **Steve Zelle**
- CLIENT **Processed Identity**

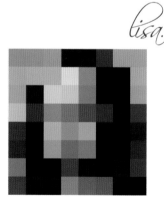

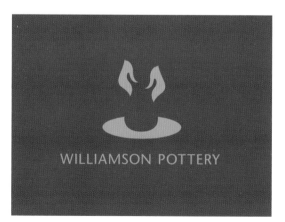

Lisa

- FIRM **Webcore Design**, South Shields, Tyne & Wear, UK
- CREATIVE TEAM **Daniel Evans**
- CLIENT **Lisa Art Blog**

Williamson Pottery Identity

- FIRM **Hayes Image**, East Geelong, Victoria, Australia
- CREATIVE TEAM **Josh Hayes**
- CLIENT **Williamson Pottery**

I LUV FLORA

"2010 was the first time that the Taipei International Flora Exposition was held in Taiwan. Taipei is the seventh city in Asia to host such a gardening expo, and this was a chance for Taiwan to show the world its commitment to outstanding gardening and the achievements it has made in the biotechnology sector. At this occasion, Human Paradise Studio was commissioned by Far Eastern Apparel Ltd. in Taiwan for a branding project. It all started from the name, which was inspired by the Taipei Flora Expo: I LUV FLORA. For the logo design, the idea came from the traditional Chinese paper-cut window frames, and FLORA's 'O'—with the Eastern philosophy of yin and yang. This was turned into a flower shape with a bird shape hidden in its very heart. We choose the unique Taiwanese native flower Pleione Formosana to be the star, combined with other Phalaenopsis flowers, birds, plants, and picture books to be displayed on several products, including clothing, stationery, and household items." —BT

- FIRM **Human Paradise Studio**, Taipei, Taiwan, China
- CREATIVE TEAM **Brad Tzou**
- CLIENT **Far Eastern Apparel Ltd.**

Ohio State Athletics Brand

- FIRM **Rickabaugh Graphics**, Gahanna, OH, USA
- CREATIVE TEAM **Eric Rickabaugh, Dave Cap, Mike Smith**
- CLIENT **The Ohio State University**

Home for the Games

- FIRM **Seven25. Design & Typography**, Vancouver, BC, Canada
- CREATIVE TEAM **Isabelle Swiderski, Setareh Shamdani**
- CLIENT **Home for the Games**

PLAY

- FIRM **Kliment**, Sofia, Bulgaria
- CREATIVE TEAM **Kliment Kalchev**
- CLIENT **PLAYER**

Granada´s Millenium

- FIRM **Valladares Diseño y Comunicación**, Santa Cruz, Spain
- CREATIVE TEAM **José Jiménez Valladares**
- CLIENT **Granada's Council**

UNRESERVED
AMERICAN INDIAN
FASHION AND
ART ALLIANCE

Unreserved

- FIRM **The O Group**, New York, NY, USA
- CREATIVE TEAM **Jason B. Cohen**, **J. Kenneth Rothermich**
- CLIENT **Unreserved American Indian Fashion and Art Alliance**

LOUD Scholarship Foundation

- FIRM **Seven25. Design & Typography**, Vancouver, BC, Canada
- CREATIVE TEAM **Isabelle Swiderski**
- CLIENT **The Gay & Lesbian Business Association of BC**

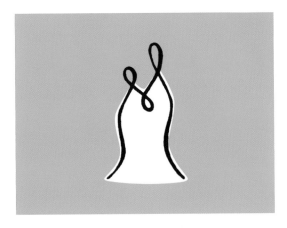

Maria Videtta

- FIRM **Southpaw Studio**, Norfolk, VA, USA
- CREATIVE TEAM **Ivanete Blanco**
- CLIENT **Maria Videtta**

Spasiba

- FIRM **Tim Bjørn – Design Studio**, Copenhagen, Denmark
- CREATIVE TEAM **Tim Bjørn**
- CLIENT **Spasiba**

- Brown's Brewing Co.

- "Brown's Brewing Company is a craft brewing pioneer. The category has taken off, and now accounts for over five percent of total industry sales. It's extremely fragmented, localized, and awash with small brands. Although Brown's beer and restaurant had won numerous regional and national awards, their distribution had been largely constrained to Troy, NY. Since 1993, this company had undergone several name changes, and prior to the rebrand, was named the Troy Pub & Brewery. As a result, brand schizophrenia was in full force. id29 renamed the brand & developed a new identity, packaging, website, and signage from the ground up that paid tribute to the rich history of brewing, but had a forward look and feel." —DB

- FIRM **id29**, Troy, NY, USA
- CREATIVE TEAM **Doug Bartow, Michael Fallone**
- CLIENT **Brown's Brewing Co.**

Michael Bach Gastroenterologists

- FIRM **Stapel Design**, Hattersheim am Main, Hessia, Germany
- CREATIVE TEAM **Josef Stapel**
- CLIENT **Dr. Michael Bach**

Latitudes

- FIRM **3 Advertising**, Albuquerque, NM, USA
- CREATIVE TEAM **Jesse Arneson**, **Tim McGrath**, **Sam Maclay**
- CLIENT **Latitudes**

T'ika

- FIRM **Machicao Design**, La Paz, Bolivia
- CREATIVE TEAM **Susana Machicao**
- CLIENT **T'ika Flower of Life**

Queen of Tarts

CUTTING
ROOM
FLOOR

- FIRM **Webcore Design**, South Shields, Tyne & Wear, UK
- CREATIVE TEAM **Daniel Evans**
- CLIENT **Queen of Tarts**

■ ■ ■

Wanderlust

"Wanderlust, as the dictionary defines, is a strong, innate desire to travel. This custom made logotype expresses the feeling of dreaminess, fantasy, and the discovery of the surreal landscape of a new world. The dash lines evoke the impulse to join the lines, as with the impulse to travel. The act of joining the lines is also analogous with the marking of lines from point to point, like a traveler would do on his map to plan/track a route. The airmail tricolor band is synonymous with traveling and correspondence—the conveyance of the emotions and thoughts kindled during a journey via mail." —YY

■ FIRM **Foreign Policy Design Group**, Singapore, Singapore
■ CREATIVE TEAM **Yah-Leng Yu**, **Tianyu Isaiah Zheng**, **Cheryl Chong**
■ CLIENT **Wanderlust Hotel**

The airmail tricolor band is synonymous with traveling and correspondence—the conveyance of the emotions and thoughts kindled during a journey via mail.

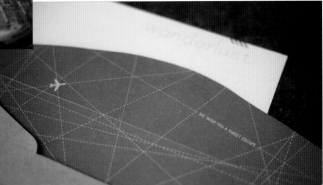

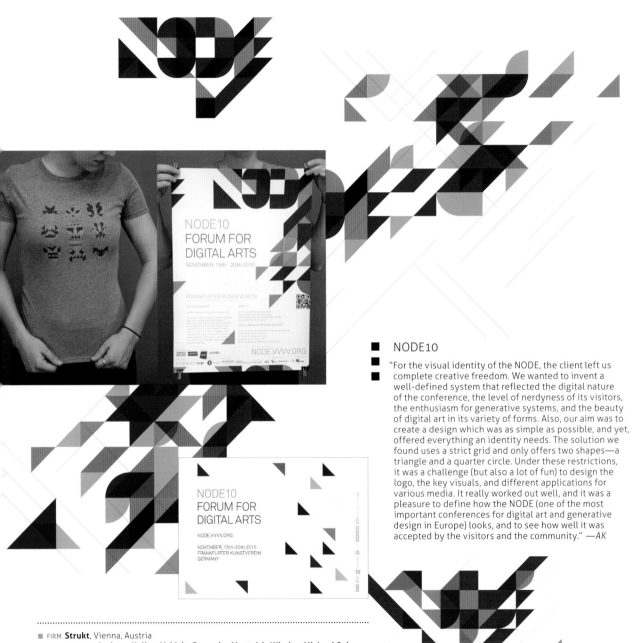

NODE10

"For the visual identity of the NODE, the client left us complete creative freedom. We wanted to invent a well-defined system that reflected the digital nature of the conference, the level of nerdyness of its visitors, the enthusiasm for generative systems, and the beauty of digital art in its variety of forms. Also, our aim was to create a design which was as simple as possible, and yet, offered everything an identity needs. The solution we found uses a strict grid and only offers two shapes—a triangle and a quarter circle. Under these restrictions, it was a challenge (but also a lot of fun) to design the logo, the key visuals, and different applications for various media. It really worked out well, and it was a pleasure to define how the NODE (one of the most important conferences for digital art and generative design in Europe) looks, and to see how well it was accepted by the visitors and the community." —*AK*

■ FIRM **Strukt**, Vienna, Austria
■ CREATIVE TEAM **Andreas Koller**, **Valérie-Françoise Vogt**, **Iris Wieder**, **Michael Seiser**
■ CLIENT **NODE Verein zur Förderung Digitaler Kultur**

ATHENS 2004

Athens 2004 Olympics

- FIRM **Red Design Consultants**, Athens, Greece
- CREATIVE TEAM **Rodanthi Senduka**
- CLIENT **Olympic Committee**

BabyDolls Boutique

- FIRM **Step Brightly Creative Group**, Oak Park, IL, USA
- CREATIVE TEAM **Lisa Guillot**
- CLIENT **BabyDolls Boutique**

Madam Madsen

- FIRM **Tim Bjørn – Design Studio**, Copenhagen, Denmark
- CREATIVE TEAM **Tim Bjørn**
- CLIENT **Madam Madsen**

cardiologic

Cardiologic

- FIRM **Hayes Image**, East Geelong, Victoria, Australia
- CREATIVE TEAM **Josh Hayes**
- CLIENT **Cardiologic**

Tawasul

■ FIRM **Storm Corporate Design**, Auckland, New Zealand
■ CREATIVE TEAM **Rehan Saiyed**
■ CLIENT **Tawasul Network Solutions LLC, Muscat, Oman**

■■ ■

The entire project was conducted via email, without any face-to-face interaction with the client.

■■ ■

Rehan Saiyed,
Storm Corporate Design

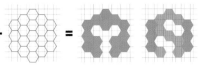

■ **Can you give us some client background?**
■ *Rehan Saiyed:* Tawasul provides e-voucher
■ payment distribution and collection solutions with software and kiosk solutions. Using Tawasul's technology solutions, people can recharge their mobile pay accounts and pay electricity, phone, water bills, etc. through standing kiosks or their mobile electronic payment system. They were founded by a team who have extensive experience in the e-payments market.

Describe the overall concept.
RS: Tawasul Electronic Network Solutions LLC wanted to rebrand itself and needed a proper design solution that reflected the company's goal to be the leading payment gateway service provider in the Middle East and North Africa. The identity needed to be used in both the Middle East and North Africa, with different names. The two needed to have enough visual similarity to appear related, but different enough to retain their individuality.

The concept included the following parts: A brand structure was developed before creating the identity, to provide clear direction for the project. I also began the project with space built in, so that if their business expanded to other Middle Eastern

countries, the design could be scalable and practical to accommodate this.

The initial concepts contained the following elements that would show up later in the final designs:

Ring Topology of Networking. In computer networking, ring topology is a configuration where each of the computers or devices are connected to each other, forming a circle or similar shape. Packets are sent around the ring until they reach the final destination. While ring topology is seldom used in current networking, the visual concept served as the basis for my designs. In fact, network topologies can take on multiple shapes or forms, but mostly, they can be categorized into the following basic types: bus, ring, star, tree, or mesh.

The identity I designed was specifically based on the ring topology. It is illustrated as a hexagon shape, with six sides. In actual ring topology, every device has exactly two neighbors for communication purposes, and I carried that visual through the concepts.

The Number Six. The principle of six is important in both structure and order, as you can see in the organized efficiency of the

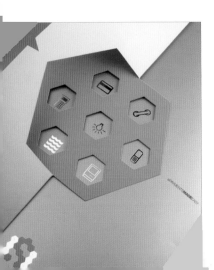

Tawasul
Electronic Network Solutions

Sahil
Electronic Services

bee and the hexagonal honeycomb it builds. Six expresses the cooperation of time, form, and energy. I also used this as the basis for developing the identity and symbol.

The Hexagon. Six shows up again in this form as well. You can see the perfect hexagonal patterns of nature in snowflakes, honeycombs, coral reefs, and the crystalline structure of diamonds. Many man-made objects that require maximum stability and strength, like six-sided faucet handles, utilize this shape as well.

The number six represents precision, and because of this, it's also found in music (the six strings of a guitar create the basis for harmony) and targeting accuracy (six bullet chambers rotate around a center pin). Multiplies of six (particularly twelve and sixty) are used to measure everyday things too: time (sixty minutes in an hour; twelve months make up a year); measurement (twelve points equals one pica; twelve inches are in a foot); and geometry (360 degrees in a circle).

In building the concept, I began with a simple grid of hexagons, and saw that connecting those hexagons could represent the concept of networking. I further simplified the grid construction to represent

more meaningful concepts and forms, like the letter "T" of Tawasul and "S" for Sahil.

What were the business and strategic goals of this project, and were they met?
RS: The official launch of the identity elevated the look of the Tawasul brand dramatically, helping alter perceptions of the company, which now communicates a prestigious and professional organization to audiences in the Middle East.

What did you most enjoy about this project?
RS: It was great to rebrand an entire organization from the ground up, designing ▶

■ ■

In building the concept, I began with
a simple grid of hexagons, and saw
that connecting those hexagons could
represent the concept of networking.

■ ■

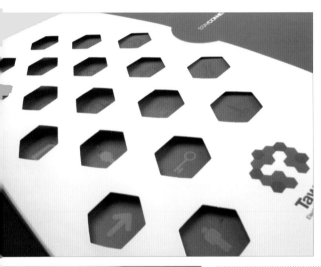

Tawasul
Electronic Network Solutions

تواصل
لخدمات الشبكات الإلكترونية

Sahil
Electronic Services

ساهل
للخدمات الالكترونية المحدودة

everything—print, digital, signage, etc.—
covering a full spectrum of disciplines.
Now I'm in the process of designing the
interior/brand environment for their future
corporate office.

**Are there any unique or interesting stories
about this project that you'd like people to
know about?**
RS: The entire project was conducted via
email, without any face-to-face interaction
with the client. I began by designing their
corporate Flash presentation with the
previous logo and identity, and after they
gained confidence in my work and approach,
we began this project together, rebranding
the entire organization. Working remotely
with the client was the most challenging
part of the process, with different time

zones, and seeking to understand and make
allowances for the cultural differences.

This identity was also honored with a
Platinum Award in the 39th Creativity
Annual Awards, and I received really
excellent feedback form the client as we
met all of their objectives—especially,
elevating the brand image of the company.

**How did you use the qualities and
strengths of print in this project?**
RS: The printers did a great job for us.
I used die cuts, special colors, and foil to
create the entire stationary range—making
it interactive, and integrating the hexagon
concept throughout the entire print
campaign. ■

BevReview

- FIRM **Hexanine**, Chicago, IL, USA
- CREATIVE TEAM **Tim Lapetino**, **Jason Adam**
- CLIENT **BevReview**

Tennis XL

- FIRM **Seven25. Design & Typography**, Vancouver, BC, Canada
- CREATIVE TEAM **Isabelle Swiderski**
- CLIENT **Tennis XL**

Bunnytown Show

- FIRM **Epos, Inc.**, Hermosa Beach, CA, USA
- CREATIVE TEAM **Gabrielle Raumberger**, **Brandon Fall**
- CLIENT **Disney/ABC Cable Networks**

iam⦿bit

iam8bit

··

- FIRM **Hexanine**, Chicago, IL, USA
- CREATIVE TEAM **Tim Lapetino, Jason Adam**
- CLIENT **iam8bit**

Far Eastern International Bank

··

- FIRM **New York Design**, Taipei Hsien, Taiwan, China
- CREATIVE TEAM **Michael Lamson**
- CLIENT **Far Eastern International Bank**

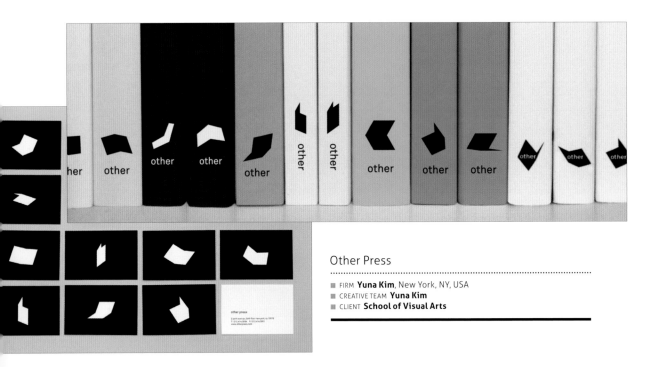

Other Press

··

- FIRM **Yuna Kim**, New York, NY, USA
- CREATIVE TEAM **Yuna Kim**
- CLIENT **School of Visual Arts**

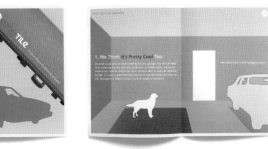

■ Dynotile

■
■ "Dynotile creates a unique and extremely durable tile product for use as a garage, hobby space, or fitness room floor covering. Once their new brand identity had been put in place, the next step was to create a handful of promotional items educating dealers and consumers about the product's key features. They also wanted to be able to send out product samples, but were leery of paying expensive production costs for slick shipping boxes that may, or may not, translate into increased sales. The solution: take advantage of a local pizza box maker. Inexpensive cardboard kept costs to a minimum, and a small die-cut window coupled with the brand's distinct orange color, resulted in a custom look that was unmistakably Dynotile." —KN

■ FIRM **Niedermeier Design**, Seattle, WA, USA
■ CREATIVE TEAM **Kurt Niedermeier**
■ CLIENT **Dynotile**

Intava

- FIRM **Niedermeier Design**, Seattle, WA, USA
- CREATIVE TEAM **Kurt Niedermeier**
- CLIENT **Intava Corporation**

Epro

- FIRM **Webcore Design**, South Shields, Tyne & Wear, UK
- CREATIVE TEAM **Daniel Evans**
- CLIENT **Epro**

Minimum

- FIRM **Kliment**, Sofia, Bulgaria
- CREATIVE TEAM **Kliment Kalchev**
- CLIENT **minimum**

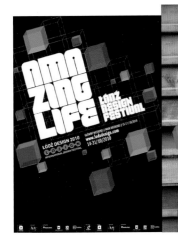

■ ■ ■

Łódź Design Festival

"We were invited by Łódź Art Center to participate in a competition for visual identification of Design Festival—LDZIGN 2010. Amazing Life was one of the first projects that challenged our creativity in creating a complex visual identity for a big event. Creating a completely new typeface, especially for this project, was something new for us, too. We wanted to highlight the main idea of Łódź Design Festival—the extraordinary life of ordinary things. We wanted our projects to show the emotions connected with the slogan of the festival, 'Amazing Life,' where color bursts through gray, and amazing life goes on around us. That's why we used unusual print techniques like 3D, colorful foil, and plexiglass." —MD

■ FIRM **Ortografika**, Lodzkie, Poland
■ CREATIVE TEAM **Marcin Dabrowski**, **Joanna Namyslak**
■ CLIENT **Lodz Design Festival**

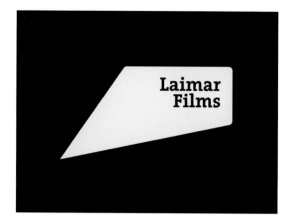

Music & Bounce

- FIRM **Erwin Hines**, San Diego, CA, USA
- CREATIVE TEAM **Erwin Hines**
- CLIENT **Music & Bounce**

Laimar Films

- FIRM **Zorraquino**, Bilbao, Spain
- CREATIVE TEAM **Miguel Zorraquino**, **Miren Sánchez**
- CLIENT **Laimar Films**

Ursa Major, Super Natural Skincare Campaign

- FIRM **Ptarmak, Inc.**, Austin, TX, USA
- CREATIVE TEAM **JR Crosby**, **Zach Ferguson**, **Sarah Emmons**, **Ben Hansen**
- CLIENT **Ursa Major**

MOKA

- FIRM **13thirtyone Design**, Hudson, WI, USA
- CREATIVE TEAM **Angela Ferraro-Fanning**
- CLIENT **MOKA**

Sheryl Crow

- FIRM **Rickabaugh Graphics**, Gahanna, OH, USA
- CREATIVE TEAM **Eric Rickabaugh**, **Dave Cap**
- CLIENT **Self-Promotion**

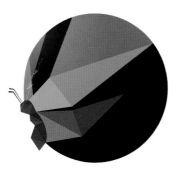

PG Moth

- FIRM **projectGRAPHICS.EU**, Prishtina, Kosova, Albania
- CREATIVE TEAM **Armelina Hasani**, **Agon Çeta**
- CLIENT **Self-Promotion**

Jazz

- FIRM **HollyDickensDesign, Inc.**, Chicago, IL, USA
- CREATIVE TEAM **Holly Dickens**
- CLIENT **Undisclosed**

BALKAN

- FIRM **Kliment**, Sofia, Bulgaria
- CREATIVE TEAM **Kliment Kalchev**
- CLIENT **Electrecords**

Stopsky's Deli

- FIRM **Sudduth Design Co.**, Austin, TX, USA
- CREATIVE TEAM **Toby Sudduth**
- CLIENT **Stopsky's Deli**

CUTTING
ROOM
FLOOR

BeautyCravings

- FIRM **HollyDickensDesign, Inc.**, Chicago, IL, USA
- CREATIVE TEAM **Holly Dickens**
- CLIENT **Victoria's Secret**

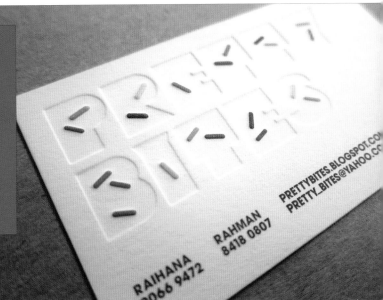

Pretty Bites

- FIRM **TRUST**, Park House, Singapore
- CREATIVE TEAM **TRUST**
- CLIENT **Pretty Bites**

Jeti Snowboarding Club

- FIRM **Andrea Zeman**, Zagreb, Croatia
- CREATIVE TEAM **Andrea Zeman**
- CLIENT **Jeti Snowboard Club**

Bistroen

- FIRM **Tim Bjørn – Design Studio**, Copenhagen, Denmark
- CREATIVE TEAM **Tim Bjørn**
- CLIENT **Bistroen KBH**

CUTTING
ROOM
FLOOR

Poop

- FIRM **Webcore Design**, South Shields, Tyne & Wear, UK
- CREATIVE TEAM **Daniel Evans**
- CLIENT **Perros Calientes**

HazCom

- FIRM **Hazen Creative, Inc.**, Chicago, IL, USA
- CREATIVE TEAM **Shawn Hazen**
- CLIENT **Self-Promotion**

Westboro Nursery School

- FIRM **idApostle**, Ottawa, AL, Canada
- CREATIVE TEAM **Steve Zelle**
- CLIENT **Westboro Nursery School**

Hype Magazine

- FIRM **João Ricardo Machado**, Caldas da Rainha, Portugal
- CREATIVE TEAM **João Ricardo Machado**
- CLIENT **Hype Magazine**

■ FIRM **Sudduth Design Co.**, Austin, TX, USA
■ CREATIVE TEAM **Toby Sudduth**, **Blue Hopkins**
■ CLIENT **Deep Eddy Spirits**

■ Deep Eddy Sweet Tea

■ "This logo is virtually the same as the final version,
■ except the girl's expression is so much more
■ inviting, cute, sexy, and memorable." —*TS*

- Perkins+Will Innovation
- Generation Campaign

- "How do you pay tribute to 75 years of design innovation? By remembering your roots, for starters. From the firm's humble beginnings, Perkins+Will has built a global, interdisciplinary practice around improving how people live, work, and learn. To help celebrate the firm's seventy-fifth anniversary, 50,000feet helped the world's largest sustainable design firm take a year-long look at the ideas and ideals that will lead us into the next 75 years and beyond. Our team partnered with Perkins+Will to deliver an integrated global communications program that included the development of a series of books, videos, and events as well as a website to host videos and content, facilitate blogging, and encourage conversation." —TW

- FIRM **50,000feet, Inc.**, Chicago, IL, USA
- CREATIVE TEAM **Jim Misener**, **Mike Petersen**, **Tracy West**, **Anthony Zinni**, **Garret Bodette**
- CLIENT **Perkins+Will**

■ HealthySpot Environmental Design

■ "As an eco-friendly and community centered venue,
■ HealthySpot wanted to raise the bar with their second store.
The widespread use of rich graphics brings out the playful side
of nature, creating a distinct and unique environment." —SWM

■ FIRM **AkarStudios**, Santa Monica, CA, USA
■ CREATIVE TEAM **Sean W. Morris**
■ CLIENT **HealthySpot**

I loved the idea that my work would be made into functional plates, mugs, and accessories.

Fishs Eddy Bridge & Tunnel Collection

"After visiting Fishs Eddy in NYC, I fell in love with the store and its whole vibe. I approached them and asked if I could design a collection for the store, and they came back with the idea to design a collection featuring all the bridges and tunnels of New York City. I was super excited because I had never worked on this sort of project before, and loved the idea that my work would be made into functional plates, mugs, and accessories. The results of the Bridge & Tunnel Collection were great, and to this date, this is one of the projects that I'm most proud of." —AB

■ FIRM **Ana Benaroya**, Jersey City, NJ, USA
■ CREATIVE TEAM **Ana Benaroya, Julie Gaines, Sara Mills**
■ CLIENT **Fishs Eddy**

■ Deathpickle

"Deathpickle started as a quick sketch at the end of a work day, and became this great little illustration that everyone seems to love. The inspiration was the white bite-mark taken out of a pickle, which simplified into a skull face. The milky, wide eyes reminded me of 'Death' from Jim Henson's *The Storyteller* series, and voilà! The character became this slavering maniac who stalks your refrigerator." —WH

■ FIRM **Sir William Wesley**, Chicago, IL, USA
■ CREATIVE TEAM **Will Hobbs**
■ CLIENT **Self-Promotion**

Kali's "Little Golden Book" Illustration

"Kali, the destroyer of men, the devourer of time. Not the best choice for a Little Golden Book, but she does make a fun Mary Blair style illustration. I draw my illustrations by hand, scan them, and then color them in Photoshop." —MRB

■ FIRM **Mike R. Baker**, Long Beach, CA, USA
■ CREATIVE TEAM **Mike R. Baker**
■ CLIENT **Self-Promotion**

mike r. baker

MOMA Bauhaus Website

"We partnered with the MoMA to design and build a companion web site and kiosk experience for the exhibition *Bauhaus 1919–1933: Workshops for Modernity*. The Bauhaus, established in Germany in the early twentieth century, still influences design, art, and architecture today. By utilizing a grid—one of the fundamental design elements of the Bauhaus—we were able to present the artists and artworks in a structured, systematic fashion. A selection of snapshots taken during the era offers an inside look into life at the Bauhaus, while a set of behind the scenes videos provides a glimpse into the effort that was involved in the preparation of the exhibition." —DL ■ *moma.org/interactives/exhibitions/2009/bauhaus*

■ FIRM **Hello Design**, Culver City, CA, USA
■ CREATIVE TEAM **David Lai**, **Hiro Niwa**
■ CLIENT **Museum of Modern Art**

■ ■ ■

Bookshape Bookcase

"This product is a synthesis of my aim as a designer: to give shape to thoughts. Bookshape is a book-containing-object (its dimensions are 60 x 60 x 12cm) where the spaces for storing the books look like the casts of an unpredictable series of volumes. Bookshape consists of a series of acrylic layers—the inner ones are white opal and exterior ones are transparent and colored. All of these layers are laser-cut in order to get a bookcase whose shape is defined by the books, because the original idea was that the content needed to give shape to its container." —DR

....

- ■ FIRM **Davide Radaelli design & music**, Milano, Italy
- ■ CREATIVE TEAM **Davide Radaelli**
- ■ CLIENT **Gspot – fabbrica di design contemporaneo**

■ ■ ■

Adidas B-Boy

"I really liked this project because there was a lot of artistic freedom, and the design was targeted towards teens with an old school hip hop theme. I wanted show the fun quality through the design, so I created a fun-loving character to express the fun of music and the movement of dancing. I also love the fact that this is a T-shirt design, because for me, T-shirt designs always seem to have a second life—first you design with the fabric color as the background, but then the shirt design interacts with other clothing and the person's environment. " —JT

....

- ■ FIRM **Studio Stubborn Sideburn**, Seattle, WA, USA
- ■ CREATIVE TEAM **Junichi Tsuneoka**
- ■ CLIENT **Adidas**

■ ■ ■

Crate & Barrel World Headquarters, Signage & Wayfinding Program

"When we started designing this signage program, we struggled to hit on a 3D sign shape that caught the spirit of this iconic contemporary housewares retailer. Then it hit us—base the sign forms on Crate & Barrel's distinctive packaging! Everything fell into place after that. The program's backbone is the monumental site ID sign that mimics a stack of Crate & Barrel gift boxes. Other key signs take their formal cue from the stacked boxes theme. The program's bold, black typography on white fields reflects Crate & Barrel's clean design aesthetic. Another design firm later knocked off our stacked boxes concept when they designed a shopping mall sign program, but they didn't pull it off as well as we did." —*CC*

■ FIRM **Calori & Vanden-Eynden**, New York, NY, USA
■ CREATIVE TEAM **Chris Calori**, **David Vanden-Eynden**, **Denise Funaro-Psoinos**
■ CLIENT **Crate & Barrel**

> This image is a reminder to me of how accidents can often be happy, and how a great image doesn't get boring.

TokyOH!

"As someone who spends the vast majority of my time looking at a screen, it can sometimes be frustrating to find a complete disparity between the flippant and sloppy joy you can get from working in a sketchbook, and the cold restraint of working on a computer. This is one of the first images I made where I felt I had found ways of working that served to blur the line between accidental and digital. It's still the image I look at to gauge whether or not I'm hitting the mark in terms of my own visual language, because I made it very quickly and yet it still has a very physical effect on my eyes and brain when I look at it. This image is a reminder to me of how accidents can often be happy and how a great image doesn't get boring." —DS

■ FIRM **Dan Stafford Illustration**, London, UK
■ CREATIVE TEAM **Dan Stafford**
■ CLIENT **Self-Promotion**

Fuck Up: A Test Print Exhibition

"This is a promo print that was created as a collaborative commemorative piece for the 2010 *Fuck Up Test Print Exhibition*. Each of the 15 artists in the show sent one randomly-selected layer of a screen printed poster which was combined together in a haphazard and chaotic print, in essence creating a new test print. One final sixteenth color featuring the show information was designed and printed over the rest of the mess." —*EN*

FIRM **Doe Eyed**, Lincoln, NE, USA
CREATIVE TEAM **Eric Nyffeler**, **Michael Nielsen**
CLIENT **Self-Promotion**

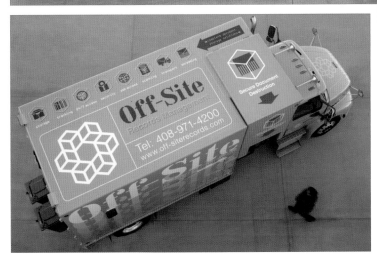

■ ■ ■

Off-Site Shred Truck Graphics

"Off-Site Records Management provides a complete range of document storage and retrieval services. Our design uses the company's descriptive name and gradation to create a metaphor for customers moving their documents 'off-site.' The shredder mechanism is highlighted in orange. The graphics showcase the symbol on one side and the company name on the other. The top functions as a dimensional billboard to display the firm's complete range of document storage solutions. The logo's dimensional boxes suggest space and storage, forming a circle to represent the access, retrieval, and linking of information." —EG

■ FIRM **Gee + Chung Design**, San Francisco, CA, USA
■ CREATIVE TEAM **Earl Gee**
■ CLIENT **Off-Site Records Management**

GIVE GREAT SERVICE

INTRODUCING *Total Service*, THE CUSTOMER SERVICE PROGRAM THAT INCLUDES EVERYONE.

EARN GREAT STUFF

INTRODUCING *Total Return*, THE EMPLOYEE REWARD PROGRAM THAT LETS YOU CHOOSE YOUR OWN AWARDS.

Experience more than 3,000 awards specifically chosen to honor your achievements and inspire you to reach even greater heights. Choose from top brands in merchandise and exclusive event and travel experiences.

CAESARSTOTALRETURN.COM

GIVE GREAT SERVICE

EARN GREAT STUFF

Caesars Entertainment Employee Rewards Campaign

"Employee engagement campaigns typically fall under the domain of HR specialists and involve little more than shotgun emails. Caesars Entertainment, the world's largest casino entertainment company, had bigger ideas. They wanted to launch a new customer service rewards program for their 25,000 employees working at 35 different properties. They wanted to excite, engage, and invigorate their team. Caesars turned to Hatch for help with virtually every aspect of the integrated communications campaign. Hatch not only named the program 'Total Service, Total Rewards,' but also created posters, a website, direct mail, table toppers, self-service kiosks, and even a 'Price is Right' game show idea to help managers introduce the new program." —KJ

■ FIRM **Hatch Design**, San Francisco, CA, USA
■ CREATIVE TEAM **Katie Jain**, **Joel Templin**, **Ryan Meis**
■ CLIENT **Caesars Entertainment**

GIVE GREAT SERVICE

INTRODUCING *Total Service,* THE CUSTOMER SERVICE PROGRAM THAT INCLUDES EVERYONE.

Total Service is our promise to customers, and to each other, to exceed expectations and continue creating a competitive advantage through excellence in service.

EARN GREAT STUFF

INTRODUCING *Total Return,* THE EMPLOYEE REWARD PROGRAM THAT LETS YOU CHOOSE YOUR OWN AWARE

Experience more than 3,000 awards specifically chosen to honor your achievements and inspire you to reach even greater heights. Choose from top brands in merchandise and exclusive event and travel experiences.

The Music Teacher

"I love this particular project because of the simplicity in which the idea was communicated. Everything is flat and minimal. The story was about a music teacher who falls in love with a student, so the combination of the trumpet with a sexy leg coming out of the horn was fun to illustrate." —AS

- FIRM **ASHKAHN Studio + Co.**, Los Angeles, CA, USA
- CREATIVE TEAM **Ashkahn Shahparnia**
- CLIENT **Jacques Magazine**

When someone puts it on, the face can have varied expressions, depending on how it's pulled onto the foot.

Beard Socks

"For this project I was given free reign to design the most awesome pair of socks ever! The one thing Ken told me to think about was to design something sculptural, since the sock would be worn on a foot. My first idea was to create the head of a bearded man. I kept it decorative and simple, but still recognizable as a face. When someone puts it on, the face can have varied expressions, depending on how it's pulled onto the foot, and also on how the foot moves. I personally love crazy socks, so this project was a dream come true!" —AB

- FIRM **Ana Benaroya**, Jersey City, NJ, USA
- CREATIVE TEAM **Ana Benaroya**, **Ken Macy**
- CLIENT **AshiDashi**

■ ■ ■

Nike "Just Do It." T-Shirt

"It was a great experience to have a client like Nike. I created illustrated typography of the 'Just Do It' slogan for this Nike Foot Locker T-shirt design. The team gave me a great deal of creative freedom, and 'Just Do It' basically says it all." —KK

■ FIRM **Kliment**, Sofia, Bulgaria
■ CREATIVE TEAM **Kliment Kalchev**
■ CLIENT **Nike**

Larkburger New Business Pitch Brochure

■ FIRM **Barnhart**, Denver, CO, USA
■ CREATIVE TEAM **Jim Hargreaves**, **Joel Hill**, **Darren Brickel**, **Teresa Brown**, **Jim Glynn**
■ CLIENT **Self-Promotion**

■ ■

This is definitely the only piece we've ever printed directly onto garbage.

■ ■

Jim Hargreaves,
Designer, Barnhart (previous)

■ **How did this project come about?**
■ *Jim Hargreaves:* Larkburger, an eco-friendly
■ and 100 percent natural burger joint, was
getting ready to open a new location in
downtown Denver. Barnhart developed this
as a new business promotion in the hopes of
landing them as a client. We wanted to design
a piece that showed we truly understood the
client and their mission, and one that would
also reflect our own passion for sustainable
design. Using reclaimed materials for the
booklet was the clear solution.

Describe the concept and how you tackled it.
JH: We figured that a city guide would
be a nice way to welcome Larkburger to
town. The piece was uniquely devised
with Larkburger's interests in mind: it
had an urban gardens map, bike routes, a
competition directory, and of course, some
information about our firm.

We had about two days to turn the entire
piece around, so there really wasn't time to
develop a brief. I guess you could say the
brief was "make something cool, and make
it quick." We did decide early on, though,
that the piece had to speak to Larkburger's
environmental philosophy.

We had visited the restaurant's flagship
location a couple times and quickly noticed
that the walls were made of reclaimed wood.
It didn't take long to realize that the booklet
should be produced in a similar way.

The entire booklet was laser printed
onto handmade sheets of paper that we
assembled from used fast-food bags,
newspaper, sandwich wrappers, and various
pieces of junk mail. Printing and assembly of
the whole piece happened in about one day,
at virtually no cost.

How did this unique process unfold?
JH: After a very quick internal brainstorm,
the first thing we did was collect all of the
used paper that would eventually become
our printing surface. I knew the design
would be simple. Given the tight deadline,
getting the materials was a bigger priority.

We basically gathered the materials from
our everyday surroundings—wrappers from
the corner coffee shop, newspapers sitting
at the front desk, junk mail on our desks—
that normally would just get trashed. ▶

For a few minutes
I was almost certain
that I had just destroyed
a $15,000 laser printer.

To court Larkburger for prospective
business, Barnhart designed
a cheeky welcome book, and
printed it on a combination of fast
food wrappers, paper, and other
reclaimed materials.

THUNDERBIRD

The authenticity of Barnhart's promo book spoke directly to Larkburger's commitment to the environment and sustainable design.

I mainly looked for pieces with interesting textures and graphics, but we also had to find materials that would be pliable enough to assemble into large sheets and run through a laser printer. When we had enough material, we were ready to go.

We already knew what basic content we wanted to include in the book. I started the page layout process while our copywriter worked on some lines. It was very much a parallel process—with only two days at our disposal, it had to be.

What was your favorite part of the project?
JH: It was really exciting to see the pages as they came out of the laser printer. The underlying patterns, text, and images on all of the wrappers and newspaper interacted with the design on top and created a real visual dynamic. Seeing everything blend together was a lot of fun.

The whole printing process was really dependent on chance too. Making the sheets was quite tedious, so there was only one chance to print each spread. We had to live with whatever layering effects we got. There's an interesting freedom in that sort of randomness and restriction.

What were your goals for this pitch project, and Larkburger's reaction?
JH: Simply put, we loved the client's product and philosophy and wanted to get them on our roster. The piece was well received, but as often happens, poor timing kept us from securing any additional work.

Tell us a little bit more of your prospective client's story.
JH: Larkburger was one of many restaurants to jump into the craft burger movement a few years ago. They use exceptional

ingredients, prepared simply and served in a sustainable setting. Their commitment to the environment and sustainable design are authentic, so we knew our promo had to be authentic as well. We also had the added difficultly of not actually having them as a client.

We wanted to present the client with something that was authentic with regard to their philosophy. It would have been easy to just print the piece on virgin stock, but that would have been contrary to everything Larkburger is trying to do. We also knew that doing something unique would have far more impact, which is worth the extra effort.

Why does this entry stand out from other work you've done?
JH: This is definitely the only piece we've ever printed directly onto garbage. Hopefully it won't be the last. This is also the only piece where I can truly say that the layout itself reacts organically to the material it was printed on. With most projects, you simply choose a paper stock, color, weight, and maybe some special inks, but here there's a visual dance that goes beyond the typical ink/paper relationship.

From a design standpoint, the piece proved to me that the best concepts tend to be the simplest. Assembling the piece was somewhat tricky, but the formula—as far as message and design—was really basic. Getting your hands dirty can be a really good thing, too. The layout was rather simple but the materials truly brought the piece to life and created something that was visually exciting.

As a firm, I think this solidified our commitment to tailor-made new business promos. They speak to the client much more than a

URBAN GARDENS:

THEY PROBABLY DON'T GROW ENOUGH VEGETAB
FOR YOUR NEEDS. BUT THERE'S GOTTA BE A GR
SPONSORSHIP OPPORTUNITY HERE.

typical capabilities piece, and you also get a bigger creative reward out of it—we were able to push our thinking, try new things, and add something really great to our portfolio.

Describe the most challenging aspect of pulling this all together.
JH: Each material presented its own challenges. The newsprint, for example, was so thin that I had to back it with another sheet before running it through the laser printer—otherwise, it would simply jam the machine or tear. The sandwich wrappers were also pretty unpredictable; most were treated with some kind of coating that didn't always react well to the heat of the laser printer. But as you can see on the cover, it resulted in some pretty cool cracking and warping.

I tried printing some of the book on Tyvek—and luckily managed to yank it out of the laser printer when it jammed. Tyvek has synthetic fibers which basically melted inside the printer. For a few minutes I was almost certain that I had just destroyed a $15,000 machine.

You chose to create a physical, printed piece for this effort rather than using interactive tools or some other method. What do you believe are the advantages of print versus other media?
JH: I think print (especially if it's a good design) forces you to sit down with it—to really spend some time with it, and engage. There's a process that happens when you have something in your hands that just can't be recreated in a screen environment. I think the audience subconsciously recognizes the effort that goes into a piece like that, and in turn, they decide to make an effort to read and explore it.

Obviously, with this piece, the magic was completely dependent on it being tangible. The design itself was rather simple—the material is what really brought interest to the page. I think it also had a great tactile quality as well, from the dry newsprint, to the waxiness of the burger wrappers, and the thick sewn binding. It was a cool booklet to hold in your hand. Definitely not something you'd throw away without thinking. ■

With most projects, you simply choose a paper stock, color, weight, and maybe some special inks, but here there's a visual dance that goes beyond the typical ink/paper relationship.

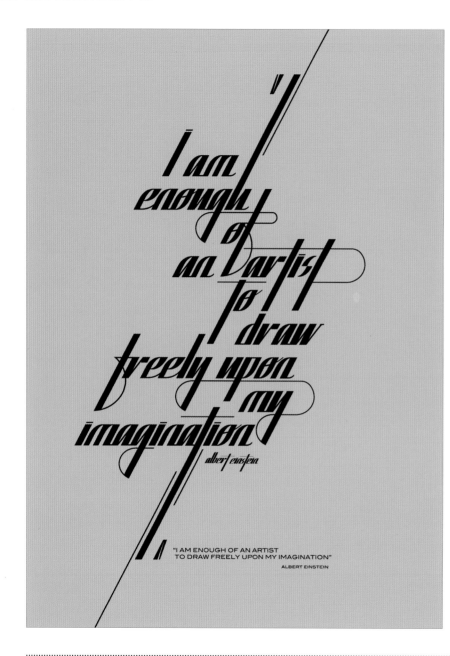

"I AM ENOUGH OF AN ARTIST
TO DRAW FREELY UPON MY IMAGINATION"
ALBERT EINSTEIN

In my opinion,
Einstein was the
same as my typeface:
a man from the future
who lived in the past.

Einstein Typeface

"This is one of my favorite projects
of all time. The main goal was to
design a special typeface for an
internal campaign in the advertising
agency I work for. I had to make a set
of posters based on typography. I
came up with this Einstein typeface.
I named it Einstein because he was
my source of inspiration. I wanted
to create a face that was retro and
new at the same time—I prefer to
call it a retrofuturistic typeface. In
my opinion, Einstein was the same
as my typeface: a man from the
future who lived in the past." —*AM*

■ FIRM **Mercury360**, Bucharest, Romania
■ CREATIVE TEAM **Alex Macsoda**
■ CLIENT **Self-Promotion**

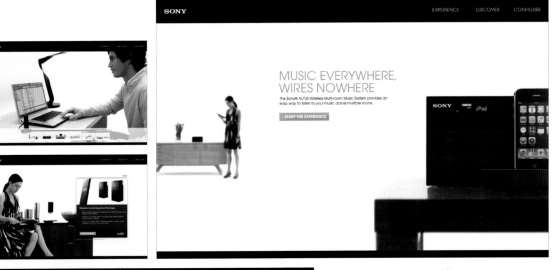

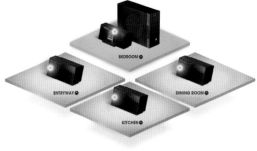

Sony Altus Microsite

"Sony's launch of the Altus wireless multi-room music system introduced a new way to enjoy music from various music devices across multiple rooms. It was one of our first fully-integrated projects where we directed a commercial shoot, designed the website, and created interactive kiosks and point-of-sale material for Best Buy and Sony Style. Our microsite showcased a couple using Altus products across different rooms in the house. Users can find detailed product features by selecting embedded hot spots. It was challenging to shoot on two sets simultaneously for both video and still photos, but we pulled it off." —DL

■ FIRM **Hello Design**, Culver City, CA, USA
■ CREATIVE TEAM **David Lai**, **Hiro Niwa**, **Sung Hean Baik**
■ CLIENT **Sony**

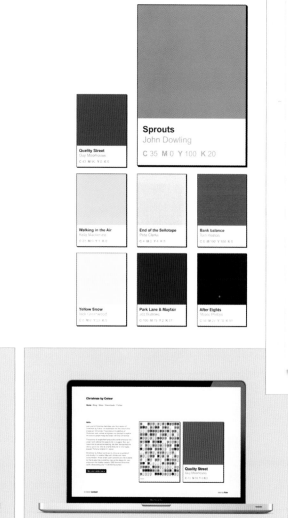

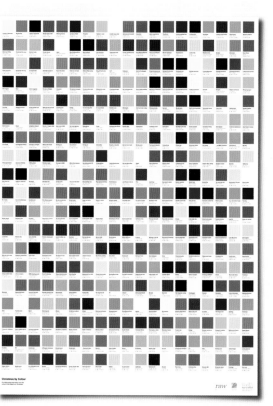

■ ■ ■

Christmas by Colour

"Christmas by Colour is a not-for-profit exploration into the colors that shape our Christmas. Frustrated at the plethora of Christmas reds, whites, and greens, we decided to explore the wider range of colors that people really associate with their Christmas. This collaborative, self-initiated project identified a diverse color spectrum, as people all over the world suggested their own color and its personal meaning. We then reviewed the entries, with the winning contributors being added to the 'nice list.' We then produced 500 Pantone-inspired A1-sized posters, which were sold via our online Christmas grotto. The success of *Christmas by Colour* was largely due to harnessing the power of blogs to attract millions of creatives." —*Ruth Sellers* ■ *christmasbycolour.co.uk*

■ FIRM **Raw Design Studio**, Salford, Greater Manchester, UK
■ CREATIVE TEAM **Rob Watson**, **Tom Heaton**, **Nick Greenwood**
■ CLIENT **Self-Promotion**

Elevate Poster

"This project was meant to serve as a catalyst for designers and artists to bring dimensionality to the flat plane. A poster is generally assumed to be flat, and is not to be altered. This invites a participant to 'introduce dimension and disrupt the surface.' Each person then photographs the volumetric version of the poster, and the image is posted in a collective exhibition at www.elevatedesign.org. The design of the poster was an interesting challenge, because of the interactive outcome I hoped for. I attempted to make the poster an intriguing and complete piece on its own, while leaving space for addition of surface variation and volume." —*KSM*

■ FIRM **thrive design**, East Lansing, MI, USA
■ CREATIVE TEAM **Kelly Salchow MacArthur**
■ CLIENT **Self-Promotion**

Beards and Trees

"I was thinking about doing a self-promotion that related to magic and the forest. This one is called 'Beards and Trees,' about a baby owl and a giant, bearded man who are friends. I'm happy with this work because it reflects the spirit of my illustration work, and I think it makes your day better." —SM

■ FIRM **Sergio Membrillas**, Valencia, Spain
■ CREATIVE TEAM **Sergio Membrillas**
■ CLIENT **Self-Promotion**

BrandScents Air Fresheners

"Is innovation in the air, or does your brand stink? At Turnstyle we asked ourselves some tough questions: What does integrity smell like? What about dedication or hard work? Should a Fortune 100 Company smell like a fortune? And what if a Fortune 1,000,000 Company smelled like a million bucks? BrandScents air fresheners produce a subtle brand impression that lingers without being overbearing. Sometimes not taking oneself to seriously is the best sell-in. This promo was a self-deprecating jab at our industry's sometimes overwrought brand babble." —SW

■ FIRM **Turnstyle**, Seattle, WA, USA
■ CREATIVE TEAM **Steven Watson**, **Ben Graham**
■ CLIENT **Turnstyle**

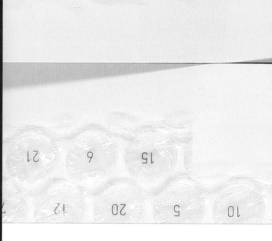

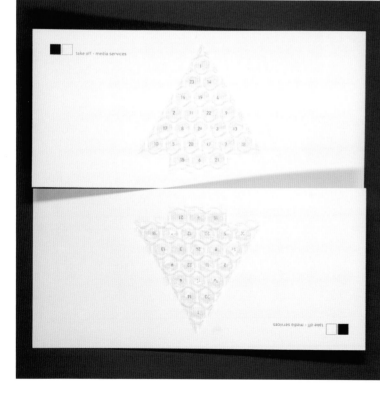

Advent Calendar

"Few people have time to appreciate all of the Christmas cards they receive each year. We designed this advent calendar as a gift to clients and friends. It's a Christmas tree cut from bubble wrap and fixed on a card with an advent calendar. So every day 'til Christmas you can pop a bubble." —CS

- FIRM **Take Off – Media Services**, Kassel, Hessen, Germany
- CREATIVE TEAM **Anna Christowzik**, **Claudius Scheuch**
- CLIENT **Self-Promotion**

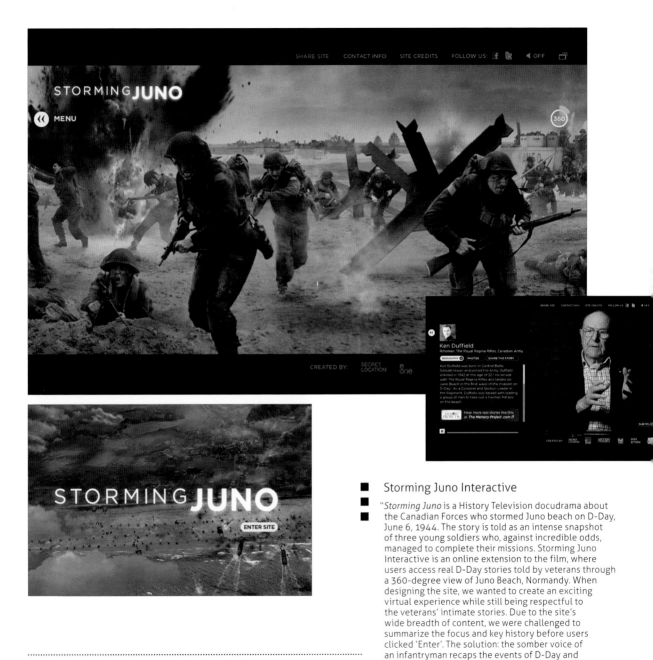

Storming Juno Interactive

"*Storming Juno* is a History Television docudrama about the Canadian Forces who stormed Juno beach on D-Day, June 6, 1944. The story is told as an intense snapshot of three young soldiers who, against incredible odds, managed to complete their missions. Storming Juno Interactive is an online extension to the film, where users access real D-Day stories told by veterans through a 360-degree view of Juno Beach, Normandy. When designing the site, we wanted to create an exciting virtual experience while still being respectful to the veterans' intimate stories. Due to the site's wide breadth of content, we were challenged to summarize the focus and key history before users clicked 'Enter'. The solution: the somber voice of an infantryman recaps the events of D-Day and introduces the real-life stories users would hear while exploring the site. " —*PG* ■ **stormingjuno.com**

■ FIRM **Secret Location**, Toronto, ON, Canada
■ CREATIVE TEAM **James Milward**, **Noora Abu Eitah**, **Pietro Gagliano**, **Ryan Andal**
■ CLIENT **History Television**

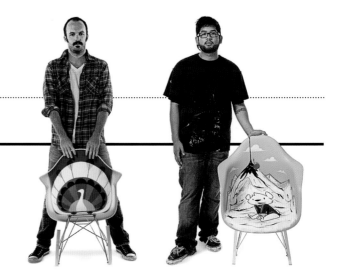

Herman Miller Design For You

hermanmiller.com/designforyou

- FIRM **Hello Design**, Culver City, CA, USA
- CREATIVE TEAM **David Lai**, **Hiro Niwa**, **Sung Hean Baik**
- CLIENT **Herman Miller**

Design for You was the first campaign we launched that placed a great deal of emphasis on the users and the power of group participation. When you put great content out there, people will seek it, spread it, and talk about it.

David Lai,
*CEO/Creative Director,
Hello Design*

Tell us how this project unfolded.

David Lai: We were in the midst of launching Herman Miller's first e-commerce store and needed to find a creative way to spread the word about the site launch. We also wanted to get people excited—this was a big initiative for the respected design brand. On a tactical level, we needed to increase Herman Miller's email list.

Describe the overall concept.

DL: Design for You was conceived as a tiered contest powered by group participation. It was also a way to showcase Herman Miller's celebrated products. In order to unlock the prizes, a targeted number of registrations were required, encouraging entrants to invite their friends and others to join.

What were the business and strategic goals of this project, and how were they met?

DL: Aside from generating buzz and building an email database, we sought to grow awareness about Herman Miller and its products. *Design for You* drew in both existing and new fans by giving away some of Herman Miller's most iconic furniture pieces, including the Eames Hang-It-All and the Embody Chair. The grand prizes, Eames

rockers painted by five selected artists, were unique to the contest. The one-of-a-kind Eames rockers sparked millions of conversations across social media platforms that continued to build momentum up to the opening of the Herman Miller online store.

We quadrupled the number of existing newsletter subscribers for Herman Miller—the contest received over 20,000 subscribers, 96 percent of which were new subscribers. We reached the 10,000-subscriber count needed to unlock all of the prizes within the first week of the contest's eight-week run.

What is the client's story?

DL: Excellent design and working for a better world around you are what define Herman Miller. The contest was a celebration of both and gave fans a chance to win these great designs and have fun while doing it.

What was your favorite part of this project?

DL: Our favorite part was working with the artists and being involved in the process of creating the grand prize Eames rockers. The artists were commissioned to paint the chairs based on the theme "for a better ▶

Hello Design partnered with Herman Miller in a competition powered by group participation. Artists expressed themselves by customizing Eames chairs which were then given away, drawing in new and existing fans.

The combination of an online campaign with physical Herman Miller products brought the whole initiative to life.

Phil Lumbang pretty much freehanded everything and although he had an idea of what he wanted to paint, he was open to just seeing where it took him. He used to work for Shepard Fairey and has done graffiti art so he was one of the first to finish.

Andrew Holder hand painted his design onto the back of the chair. He went over each area carefully with several layers of paint but when he began to run out of time, he started using a hair dryer to get the paint to dry faster.

Christopher Lee is a talented illustrator but he works mostly on the computer. This was a fun project for him because it was one of his first paintings, and on a chair no less.

What was unique about your audience?
DL: Herman Miller's audience is made up of passionate individuals from the design and A&D community. Their taste is top-notch and they expect quality from everything Herman Miller creates. In order to keep the audience interested and excited, we handpicked each prize to be given away in the contest, releasing a new prize each week.

Why was the web chosen as the medium for this project?
DL: We wanted to reach the widest audience possible and the web is where people are today. We've been immersed in digital since 1999, constantly living in it and learning new things as it evolves everyday. Today the online space and the physical world are becoming more and more intertwined. Although *Design for You* was an online campaign, we were giving away coveted products that were delivered to each winner, bringing the campaign to life. ■

Our favorite part was working with the artists and being involved in the process of creating the grand prize Eames rockers.

world around you." Although each chair was unique to the individual artist, there's a backstory that isn't immediately apparent that tied them all together.

Each of the artists was meticulous, but each had different approaches. Mark Giglio used a ruler, masking tape, and an X-Acto knife to precisely cut out his stencil so he could spray paint his design. He showed an incredible amount of patience in his prep work and didn't even begin to paint until half the day was already over. We were really impressed that he had custom measured and sewn a seat cushion for the Eames rocker in advance. The cushion fabric was his own design, of course.

Josh Cochran drew all his detailed illustrations with a pencil and then traced over his drawings again with a paintbrush—so basically he drew his design twice. We thought it was cool too that he had already planned out his drawing and referenced his sketches on his iPhone.

■ ■

It is not wrestling—
It's Lucha Libre!

■ ■

■ **Lucha Libre AAA Website**

■ "It was very bizarre that, with all the gamers working at GrupoW, we
■ could count with the fingers of one hand our experiences working
for videogames. That is why we were very exited at being reached by
Slang to develop the website for their new videogame, 'Lucha Libre
AAA: Heroes del Ring.' We thought about the *luchador* and his mask,
which is commonly viewed as the new mariachi when people talk
about Mexico. This project allowed us to explore the whole country
and the ritual of the Mexican Lucha Libre. Commonly confused with
American wrestling, it was time that a game and its website could
emphasize the differences between both sports. It's not wrestling—
it's Lucha Libre!" ■ *grupowprojects.com/slang/heroesdelring/site*

■ FIRM **GrupoW**, Mexico City, Mexico
■ INTERACTIVE AGENCY **GrupoW**
■ CLIENT **Heroes del Ring**

■ ■ ■

Georgia Max Coffee Effect

"Copy translation: 'Seriously, kick ass intensely sweet real coffee, super zinging unstoppable MAX! Energy booster!' This is an extra sweet high energy beverage made to boost energy. The brand held ski/ snow board events at major ski resorts around Japan promoting the launch of the beverage. The objective of the campaign was to maximize its presence in the market with the integrated mass media campaign. In order to gain awareness among the target audience, the toilets of these major ski resorts were turned into a ski jumper's view, giving a 'MAX' experience in the most unlikely places. We expected that users would share the experience with friends using email and social media sites, creating massive buzz." —*K. Kanazki*

■ FIRM **TUGBOAT**, Tokyo, Japan
■ CREATIVE TEAM **Kengo Kato, Koji Kanzaki**
■ CLIENT **Coca-Cola (Japan) Co., Ltd.**

■ ■ ■

Zumiez Trims & Packaging

"Zumiez develops several private label brands, including Empyre Snow, Empyre Casuals, Empyre Girls, Rälik, Alab, Aperture, and Freeworld. Hundreds of separate pieces were developed for their 2008/2009 trims and packaging—everything from zipper pulls to hangtags—and applied to everything from hoodies to snowpants. These small details not only make an ordinary piece of clothing feel special, but also serve as a point of purchase display. Hitting the right cultural touchpoints was critical, as Zumiez caters to a demographic of eleven- to twenty-four-year-olds with an interest in skate and snow culture." —*Josh Oakley*

■ FIRM **Weather Control**, Seattle, WA, USA
■ CREATIVE TEAM **Keith Walbrun**, **Christina Draper**, **Joe Windemuth**
■ CLIENT **Zumiez**

Chromolux Pure Calendar

"We created a three-dimensional wall sculpture for the fine paper company, M-real Zanders. The sculpture is also a calendar, created using only the CHROMOLUX paper line. Curved CHROMOLUX stripes in different colors and lengths represent each week of the year. The bottoms of the strips are attached to the calendar, and the tops are just slotted in. By pulling out the appropriate calendar week, the dates for that particular week are revealed with a silver foil imprint. At the end of the week, the paper strip is folded back into its original position and the next week is opened. This turns the calendar into a living, constantly changing object." —TS

■ FIRM **zinnobergruen**, Duesseldorf, Germany
■ CREATIVE TEAM **Bärbel Muhlack**, **Tobias Schwarzer**
■ CLIENT **M-real Zanders gmbh**

Paul Elledge Photography Website

"As we thought about how to present the work of photographer Paul Elledge on his website, we knew we needed to capture his spirit, personality, and creative energy. We noticed that Paul is a doodler. Every surface of his camera gear is covered with drawings and stickers. Stop by his studio and you'll notice that the drawings go beyond the camera gear, to light switches and walls. Our observations led us to an idea—that the best way to present his work was through illustration. So we took those doodles and drawings and animated them. The site became an extension of his travel gear. The doodles swim though the eight gallery numbers like sea creatures in the ocean. They become the windows you look through to experience the photo galleries." —TB ■ *paulelledge.com*

■ FIRM **lowercase**, Chicago, IL, USA
■ CREATIVE TEAM **Tim Bruce**
■ CLIENT **Paul Elledge Photography**

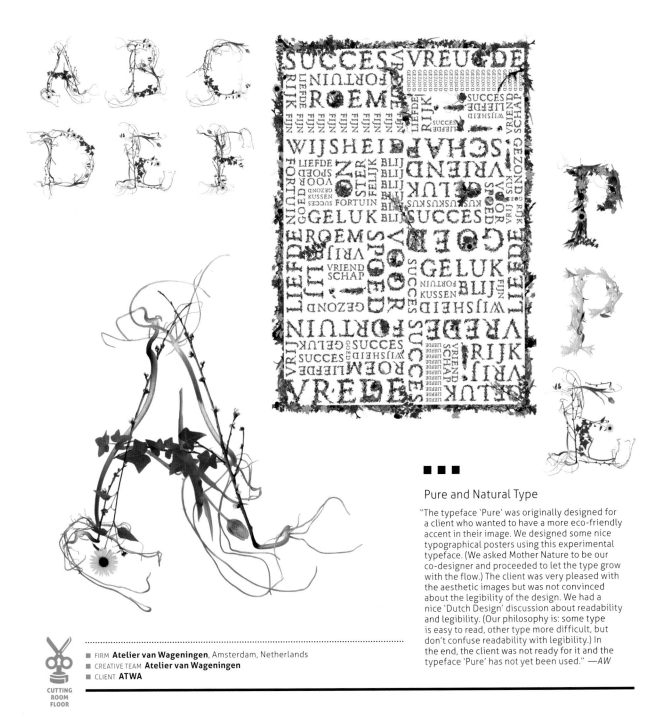

Pure and Natural Type

"The typeface 'Pure' was originally designed for a client who wanted to have a more eco-friendly accent in their image. We designed some nice typographical posters using this experimental typeface. (We asked Mother Nature to be our co-designer and proceeded to let the type grow with the flow.) The client was very pleased with the aesthetic images but was not convinced about the legibility of the design. We had a nice 'Dutch Design' discussion about readability and legibility. (Our philosophy is: some type is easy to read, other type more difficult, but don't confuse readability with legibility.) In the end, the client was not ready for it and the typeface 'Pure' has not yet been used." —AW

- FIRM **Atelier van Wageningen**, Amsterdam, Netherlands
- CREATIVE TEAM **Atelier van Wageningen**
- CLIENT **ATWA**

CUTTING
ROOM
FLOOR

■ ■ ■

Burberry Dots

"The client briefed us to develop an advertising campaign, aimed at fashionable young women in Japan, that would change Burberry's conservative and staid image. We proposed reinventing the trademark Burberry check pattern to help the brand evolve. Our intent was to make Burberry Dots the new icon that would shake up the currently stagnant fashion identity. We transformed the form and feature of the Burberry Check into dots, while maintaining the original DNA, to propel the brand into a newer, more challenging arena. Our aim was to develop products where heritage and innovation could be enjoyed simultaneously." —SK

■ FIRM **TUGBOAT**, Tokyo, Japan
■ CREATIVE TEAM **Seijo Kawaguchi**, **Bridge**
■ CLIENT **Sanyo Shokai Ltd.**

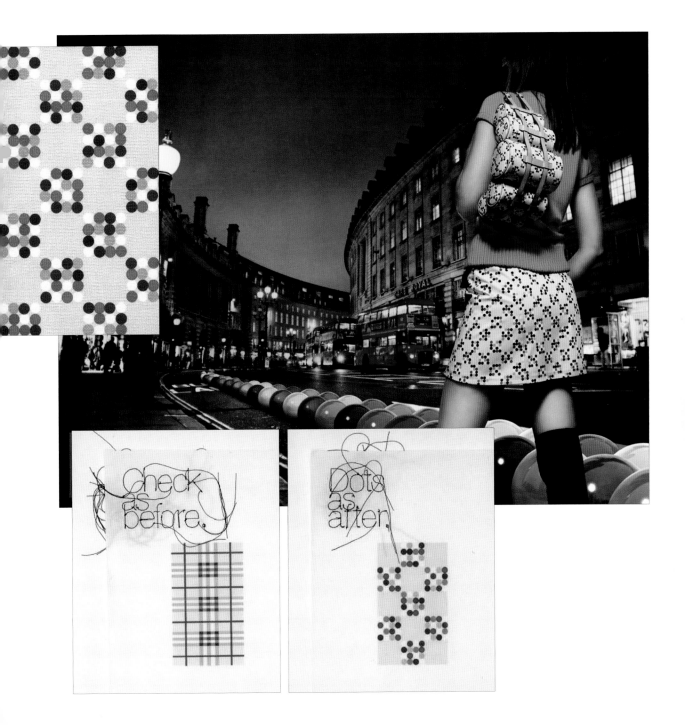

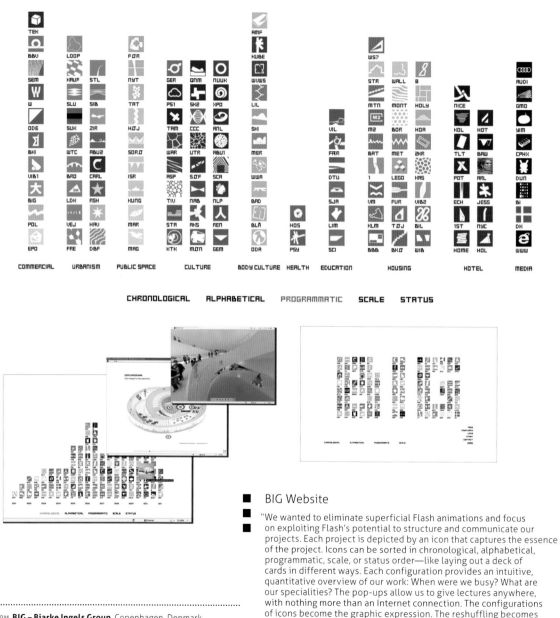

BIG Website

"We wanted to eliminate superficial Flash animations and focus on exploiting Flash's potential to structure and communicate our projects. Each project is depicted by an icon that captures the essence of the project. Icons can be sorted in chronological, alphabetical, programmatic, scale, or status order—like laying out a deck of cards in different ways. Each configuration provides an intuitive, quantitative overview of our work: When were we busy? What are our specialities? The pop-ups allow us to give lectures anywhere, with nothing more than an Internet connection. The configurations of icons become the graphic expression. The reshuffling becomes the animation. The content becomes the form." ■ **big.dk**

■ FIRM **BIG – Bjarke Ingels Group**, Copenhagen, Denmark
■ CREATIVE TEAM **Bjarke Ingels**, **Jakob Lange**, **Teis Draiby**
■ CLIENT **Self-Promotion**

Eric Steuten: Design & Concept Website

"Fresh out of a job, I was determined to get back on my feet as soon as possible, so I created a new portfolio site. I knew I had to stand out with something more than just my work, with an eye-catcher that had high recollection value. So I created the centerpiece artwork with my own professional rebirth in mind—a witty, tongue-in-cheek approach—and as a personal tribute to my own son. Humor is a great, non-invasive way into someone's cognitive memory. The story behind the work was a perfect starting point for interviews. The overwhelming response, great end result, and its underlying duality make this my favorite project to-date." —ES ■ **ericsteuten.nl**

■ FIRM **Eric Steuten**, Eindhoven, Netherlands
■ CREATIVE TEAM **Eric Steuten**
■ CLIENT **Self-Promotion**

INDEX

AUTHORS

Tim and Jason are the co-founders of Hexanine, a design firm focusing on branding and identity. Hexanine employs a blend of strategy and style to help organizations communicate their singular brand stories. The firm has offices in Chicago and Los Angeles.

Tim Lapetino

Tim is passionate about working alongside the brands that impact our culture. He currently serves as Adjunct Faculty at Chicago Portfolio School and on the AIGA Chicago Board of Directors as Co-Development Chair.

Jason Adam

Jason is devoted to solving the world's communication problems through a mix of visual beauty and thoughtful design. He currently serves on the Board of Directors of AIGA Los Angeles.

■ ■ ■